SQL

ADVANCED SQL QUERY
OPTIMIZATION TECHNIQUES

Andy Vickler

© **Copyright 2021 - All rights reserved.**

The content contained within this book may not be reproduced, duplicated or transmitted without direct written permission from the author or the publisher.

Under no circumstances will any blame or legal responsibility be held against the publisher, or author, for any damages, reparation, or monetary loss due to the information contained within this book, either directly or indirectly.

Legal Notice:

This book is copyright protected. It is only for personal use. You cannot amend, distribute, sell, use, quote or paraphrase any part, or the content within this book, without the consent of the author or publisher.

Disclaimer Notice:

Please note the information contained within this document is for educational and entertainment purposes only. All effort has been executed to present accurate, up to date, reliable, complete information. No warranties of any kind are declared or implied. Readers acknowledge that the author is not engaging in the rendering of legal, financial, medical or professional advice. The content within this book has been derived from various sources. Please consult a licensed professional before attempting any techniques outlined in this book.

By reading this document, the reader agrees that under no circumstances is the author responsible for any losses, direct or indirect, that are incurred as a result of the use of information contained within this document, including, but not limited to, errors, omissions, or inaccuracies.

Table of Contents

Introduction 1
    Understanding Databases Today 2
    Structure of this Book 4
    Database Queries 4

Chapter 1: Structured Query Language in Oracle 6
    The History of the SQL 6
    Variations in the SQL Today 8
    Procedural Language for SQL by Oracle 10
    The Syntax of PL/SQL 11
    Queries in the SQL & their Syntax 14

Chapter 2: Query Processing & Query Optimization 22
    The Phases of Query Processing 23
    Fundamentals of Query Optimization 26

Chapter 3: Query Optimization Techniques 29
    What is Optimization? 29
    What a Query Does 31
    The Tools 33
    What the Query Optimizer Does 36
    Common Query Optimization Themes 39

    Joins and WHERE Clauses Wrapped in Functions......................41

    Implicit Conversions...44

Chapter 4: Query Optimization Tips and Tricks........................... 47

    Tips and Tricks...47

Chapter 5: Using the Rule-Based Optimizer................................ 73

    Understanding the RBO Access Paths 74

    Using RBO to Choose an Execution Plan for a Join...................93

    Using the RBO to Transform and Optimize Statements...........96

    Alternative SQL Syntax...97

Chapter 6: Using the Cost-Based Optimizer and Database Statistics... 101

    DBMS_STATS...104

Chapter 7: Reading an Execution Plan 121

    What Is An Execution Plan? 122

Chapter 8: SQL Server Query Optimization Techniques 132

    Understanding the Application...133

Conclusion... 162

References 164

Introduction

At their inception, databases were nothing more than a simple system that could save a handsome number of records for an organization. This included databases for employees, customers, transactions, and the budget. Initially, these different types had to be saved separately in different databases. However, with time, these systems became more and more complex and allowed more flexibility to the database administrators and the organizations managing them. We saw the introduction of a variety of features like relations, joins, indexes, and queries. As of now, databases have proven themselves to be one of the most powerful tools in human history. From large corporate giants like Facebook and Google to small settlements like a local pharmacy or supermart, the database has evolved from a facilitative role to one of necessity. Any business that wants to guarantee its success must have a database (for the starters). Without that, its survival cannot be guaranteed at all. Moreover, organizations compete with each other with regard to data, and better and more optimized usage of the data provided to them in those databases serves as a key to their success.

Understanding Databases Today

Long gone are the days where databases were used as a means just to store necessary data. In fact, the very name database came into existence only after its being built upon Codd's model. While data storage is still an important component of database systems, it is not the only primary goal for having databases, except for home use - some individuals may have simple databases on their personal computers. Today's targeted (or wider) purpose of databases is to make sense of data by extracting the required information and putting the conclusions derived from that information to good use. This fundamental use of databases makes use of a very important concept (i.e., querying) and can be broken down into two fundamental dimensions. They are discussed below.

Database Handling for Monetization Purposes

All big organizations use databases today to further expand their businesses and generate even more revenue for themselves. Of course, this task is not as easy as it sounds and may require a lot of time and patience to benefit from. First, organizations make use of databases to store important user data. Then, that data is analyzed through time to consider the ongoing business trends that the company can use to predict their most profitable moves for the future. This is a basic technique used by all existing businesses, from Facebook to large departmental stores.

For example, Facebook keeps track of each user's activity stored in a database to determine what kind of content and advertisements should be shown to the user. This aims to increase Facebook usage time for regular users significantly, and the more someone uses this application, the more it benefits Facebook. This probably explains why you spend so much time every day needlessly scrolling your Facebook feed.

The departmental stores, likewise, do the same thing while using a starkly different approach. They may use the databases to determine what kinds of products are usually brought by the customer together. They may put them in the same place, thereby increasing the chances of both of the things being bought. The same technique is used by eCommerce sites like Amazon, where you see a list of recommended products with a product you are buying or considering buying.

You may have noticed (at least partly) that there are more things in play here, along with database handling. Those things mainly include a deep understanding of human psychology, without which the efficient use of databases cannot be ensured. Remember this point as it will be important for us in our discussion on query optimization.

Database Handling for Research Purposes

Research today is extremely dependent upon database systems. The point is to store enough data that can be processed in the future to derive important scientific conclusions. Suppose our research is in the domains of Physics or Computer Science. In that case, we may require data on a lot of calculations in a particular domain, which could be used to understand the computers' universe better, subsequently. On the other hand, if the research is in the domain of psychology or biology, we may need a record of human behavior to certain stimuli or different contexts to better facilitate the research.

These pieces of information are analyzed with different environments and circumstances at hand, and through that, researchers determine if there is any valid correspondence. Without a proper database, it would be hard to track all the contexts or determine the reason for any consequence of that research.

Structure of this Book

The structure of this book has been designed to keep all our readers involved with the book throughout the reading process, and once you have read the entire book, you will be aware of the concept of query optimization thoroughly. In Chapter #1, we give a brief intro on the Structured Query Language in the Oracle database. In Chapter #2, Query Processing will be discussed, which is an important prerequisite of query optimization. In fact, you could call query optimization the most important subset of query processing, while there may be instances where query optimization could be entirely independent of query processing.

Nevertheless, after getting a strong background in query processing, we will move on to discuss all the different ways you can optimize your SQL queries from Chapter # 3 onwards.

Database Queries

Do keep in mind that you must have substantial knowledge of database queries if you want to benefit from the book. If you do not know what queries are and the various ways they can be used, there is no point in understanding query optimization, as that is nothing but the post-requisite of database queries. The initial chapter of our book focuses on the basics of SQL and queries, so pay great attention to them. Whatever is discussed, there will be enough for you to go about this book. However, if you already have strong domain knowledge and considerable experience with Oracle SQL, you may skip the first two chapters.

Important Note for the Readers

You already know that Oracle SQL is a demonstrative language for discussing query optimization in this book. If you aim to work professionally in this language or are already working in it, that makes it the perfect book for you. However, none of that means this book is useless if you are working on some other SQL variant, like T-SQL or MySQL, or perhaps some other No-SQL database. For theoretical understanding, the things discussed here would be beneficial for you regardless of your background. Even though we discuss **the advanced** query optimization techniques, the code provided in the book will be quite simple, and anyone, regardless of their background, will be able to grasp the concepts discussed here.

Chapter 1

Structured Query Language in Oracle

The Structured Query Language, otherwise known as SQL, is the most popular language for databases today. Although its popularity has been steadily decreasing for the past few years, it is still expected to be the most widely used language for a long time. While initially, it was a standard language, it kept evolving through time and now has many variants used by different database systems. That's pretty much how living things evolved, too, through time. Nevertheless, this language has a very interesting history. The shapes and forms it is used in today, and the variety of things you can do with them are even more interesting. To initiate our discussion and clarify which variant of SQL (used in Oracle) we will be using, we will first discuss the history of the Structured Query Language. Then, we shall move on to its different variants and the basic differences between them, and finally, we will understand the syntax of Oracle SQL.

The History of the SQL

Initially, data was stored and managed throughout the world in a very inefficient way. The most well-known example is a file-handling system, which took a lot of processing time and led to much data redundancy. Moreover, that system would lead to contradictions in the stored data since it was stored in multiple places at a time. To make things worse, a change in one location had to be implemented manually everywhere. To put an end to this nuisance, Edgar F. Codd (a computer scientist working in IBM) introduced the relational model for data management. His colleagues in IBM, Boyce, and Chamberlin started working on a language for IBM's official database management system, System R.

After an initial failure with the Square Language, they finally developed the first successful database language that became known as SEQUEL, which meant Structured English Query Language. However, due to some external conflicts, it was later named SQL, a term we all know today.

Evolution of SQL through Time

SQL has traditionally been a declarative programming language. It is a paradigm wherein the flow of the program is not explained but just the declarative statements. To put it in simple terms, the system to told to perform a specific task via a program, but it is not told how the program should be executed like it is in imperative programming languages like C++ or Java. . Let's note some interesting points regarding that:

- The declarative paradigm of SQL gives us an easy methodology to extract data from memory fast and efficiently. However, it may lead to limitations.

- To cope with the limitations of declarative programming, different organizations introduced interesting extensions to SQL, giving it capabilities that hold some resemblance to the imperative paradigm.

- While the technical syntax of SQL is the same, slight variations have arisen with time. For example, Microsoft's SQL server does not require the use of semicolons while writing the code.

All these changes have gone so far and wide that one could call the SQL in one domain an entirely different language than the SQLs in other domains. Pretty much like how the basic keywords in all imperative programming languages (if statements, while loops, for loops, etc.) are the same in different programming languages. However, that is not really true since SQL, regardless of whatever variant you are using, is fundamentally the same. However, you may have to edit the code a little bit if you wish to transfer from one DBMS (Database Management System) to another.

Variations in the SQL Today

Given the vast amount of changes SQL has gone through with time and the diverse range of options that have popped up with the evolution of this language, it can get pretty hard to predict which version of the query language it is when you see one. Moreover, all the variations of this language have their own pros, cons, and strengths. To put it in other words, it is as complex as it can get, and with time the diversity will get even more complex as the language gets simpler and more user-friendly. In this section, we have discussed 2 SQL variants that are not relevant to us but are important.

Transact SQL

Sybase developed the T-SQL, and currently is in use by Microsoft in MS SQL Server. The SQL standard has been extended by T-SQL with the additional functionality of support of local variables and string processing. Moreover, string processing also becomes a possibility via T-SQL. Since this variant is propriety, in essence, no other organization can make use of this database system under their own brand name.

SQL/PSM

This variant may be better known as SQL/Persistent Stored Modules. It is a common methodology with cross-platform operating system support. Despite the name being different, the functionality and benefits of SQL/PSM do not differ that much from T-SQL or most other versions of SQL. It is currently being implemented in many famous database systems, including MySQL, MonetDB, and MariaDB.

While both of these databases are extremely powerful and popular, when it comes to fame, they are not on par with Oracle, which is the most famous database in the world. Due to Oracle's overwhelming fame, the PL/SQL it implemented also became the most famous variant of the Structured Query Language and probably the most famous database language. Only a few other databases have implemented this format for their database systems, however. We shall discuss it in detail throughout the chapter.

Procedural Language for SQL by Oracle

The non-procedural approach of SQL was seen as its biggest feature. It brought ease to people and organizations as they were free from the need to define every step or iteration in detail, and pretty much all the processing was left to the database system itself. However, as beneficial as that approach is, it sure has its limitations. Initially, it was not seen as a big deal, but time showed that changes were certainly required. The database systems could not perform many tasks, and the procedural approach had to be reintroduced to make these systems more dynamic, powerful, and versatile. The approach used by Oracle was PL/SQL. In fact, the introduction of procedural language for SQL gave Oracle a boost and made it among the top software companies in the world. It retains that status to this day.

Since we aim to delve into Query Optimization in detail, we will have to understand PL/SQL in detail. Before that, however, we should look into the key features of this language, as they will help make the different aspects of its syntax quite clear to you. Some of the key features of PL/SQL have been discussed below:

- PL/SQL is strongly integrated with SQL, making them a single entity. This strengthens the capabilities of both the SQL and the procedural language.

- The use of functions, procedures, stored procedures, and triggers are provided.

- You have a plethora of programming methodologies and uncountable types of metadata for this structure.

- You can even make powerful web applications with PL/SQL.

- PL/SQL significantly reduces the chances to compromise on security and data integrity.

The Syntax of PL/SQL

Now that we have discussed the fundamental features and advantages of PL/SQL, it would be worth looking into the syntax of this language. Throughout this book, we shall use this language to understand query optimization better, so it would be in your best interest to fully understand this language's syntax. You do not have to have a mastery of Oracle's PL/SQL, but just the fundamental understanding of it will make you good to go. Let's take our discussion sequentially.

Foundation of PL/SQL – The Block Statement

Procedural Language for SQL gives it a block structure. All the commands are executed within a block, and they can be broken down into three basic segments. They are the declarations, the executable commands, and exception handling. For example:

```
DECLARE
            ... Declare variables here ...
```

```
BEGIN
        ... Main Program ...
EXCEPTION
        ... Exception Handling ...
END;
```

You can see from the foundational syntax above that the block will culminate after the END keyword, and the keyword has to be followed by a semicolon. However, this doesn't mean that this is the only place where you will see a semicolon, as it is required elsewhere in the program. It will become clear to you in a bit.

Variable Declarations

When writing a block for PL/SQL in Oracle, the variables must be defined in the declaration section. Here you can declare or initialize as many variables as you require, and there are different ways of doing them, depending upon if you need them with values or if you only need them to exist for now. Refer to the code segment below:

```
        f_name      varchar(20);
    l_name      varchar(20) := NULL;
        num         integer := 15;
```

You can see from the code given above that the variable name (assigned by you) is given on the left-hand side. On the right side, you will specify the datatype of the named variables and may assign them values depending on your needs. Do note each of these declarations must end with a semicolon, and if you want to assign a value, you will have to use the operator ":=" which specifies that the variable contains this (or these) values. Also, note that the number in the brackets (i.e., 20) specifies the number of characters allowed at max in the case of the varchar data type above.

Exception Handling

Exception handling is a very important part of the Oracle SQL code. Do note that it may not be quite relevant to us because it has not much to do with Query Optimization, but it would still be worth discussing. Exception handling is always written in the EXCEPTION segment. The program enters this segment only if an error is found anywhere in the block above. In this segment, we direct the program on what it should do if it comes across any type of error to avoid any problem or inconvenience. Note that this segment is not mandatory in the PL/SQL block.

Inner and Outer Blocks

It is possible to have blocks within a block statement in PL/SQL. This phenomenon is called nested blocks. Even the nested blocks can have more blocks within them, and this can be taken forward as much as you like. However, note that you will be required to have a separate "END;" statement or EXCEPTION segment where required for each block statement. An example has been provided below:

```
BEGIN
    <some code>
    BEGIN
        <some code>
    END;
END;
```

It is a good practice to indent the code properly (depending on the created nests) to ensure clarity for yourself or any other user that may have access to the code. Note that the first END terminates the second BEGIN statement, and the second END terminates the first BEGIN statement. If your code is not indented, it may get hard for you to properly grasp this fact, even if you are well aware of this rule.

Condition & Loop Structures in PL/SQL

The PL/SQL also allows basic looping structures and conditions one finds in all imperative programming languages. The usage is pretty much the same, but when seen from the context of a database, these structures give additional processing power to the database and allows administrators to perform such tasks quickly with just a few lines of code, which were traditionally considered hard complex, and hectic. We don't need to discuss the syntax of these structures, but they will become apparent when you see them being used in sample codes provided in the book.

Queries in the SQL & their Syntax

So far, what we discussed in this chapter was important, but it didn't hold much relevance to our discussion on advanced query optimization in SQL. At most, the knowledge shared above will help the readers comprehend any Oracle SQL code they come across in their professional life. Now we shall discuss something that is of much more relevance and importance to us: Queries in the Structured Query Language. This section will discuss different types of queries in SQL, their purpose, and their syntax in Oracle

PL/SQL. Then in the chapters succeeding this one, we shall move on to the discussions surrounding queries and their optimization.

There are a total of 8 queries in the Oracle database. Each of these queries has its dimensions, functions, and properties, and they are integral to any database system. While some queries may hold similarities with others, like DELETE, DROP, and TRUNCATE statements. Still, they are quite different, and not all of them can necessarily be used in the same scenario. This will get obvious to you in a little while. Before that, however, we need to clarify one important thing. We have discussed the syntax of PL/SQL above, but queries need not be written in the block at all times. For that, we will have to understand the two methodologies of implementation of the queries.

Stored Procedures & Triggers

These are two very important concepts in SQL, but their importance is to the point where we need to understand where the queries can be used. Note that, in PL/SQL, you can write your queries in the blocks or outside the blocks, but that would depend on the methodology you are using to write your database. If you are making use of writing a stored procedure, then your query has to be a part of the block, and in that case, it will be written in the BEGIN statement of the block. However, in SQL, you can also make use of triggers, and in that case, the query may be written separately. However, then the code will not follow the rules of the Procedural Language but would only be a basic SQL code that neither takes an input nor returns a value.

Now let us move on to discuss all the Queries in Oracle in detail:

Create Query

The CREATE statement is used when one wants to create a database or a table mainly. If required, further information may be provided (according to the syntax) to create the table. However, once executed, you cannot alter the code in the segment. If you want to bring the relevant changes to the table, you will have to use the alter query discussed ahead. The basic syntax following the CREATE statement is given below:

```
CREATE TABLE apartments
(id          number(20) NOT NULL,
 name        varchar(30) NOT NULL,
 sq_meters   number(15),
 rent        number(5,-2)
);
```

The code above will create a table, which is one of the basic structures of a database, without where there is no point. It is through tables we excrete important information for further processing and for predicting trends. Once you have created a table, you now can insert relevant data inside the table.

Insert Query

Now that a table has been created, you will need the INSERT query to add the data. The basic syntax for an insert query is shown below:

```
INSERT INTO apartments (id, name, rent, sq_meters)
```

```
                    VALUES (001, 'Green_Villa',
        34500, 1350);
```

When executed, this statement will save the relevant information in the table. Note that after the "INTO" statement, the order has been changed, i.e., when creating the table, sq_meters was added first, but while inserting, we wrote rent first in the metadata. It will not give an error, but the values will be saved in the latter order. So, hypothetically, if 1350 was actually the apartment's rent, in the table, it will be saved in the column of sq_meters. If you happen to make this mistake, you cannot correct the values manually. For that, you will have to make use of the alter query.

Alter Query

The alter statement is probably one of the most powerful queries in any database. Using this keyword, you can perform multiple functions like changing the table columns or extending the table by adding more columns, or reducing it by removing some columns. Moreover, you can add or remove primary keys, change the data types of variables, and so on. Basic use of the alter query is used below:

```
            ALTER TABLE apartments
            ADD COLUMN property_type varchar(20);
```

The statement above has added a new column to the table. However, since it was not possible to provide data for the property_type when we were inserting it into this table above, we will have to update it if we want to add new data. If you do not do so, the value in the first row (id: 001) will remain NULL.

Update Query

The update query is a feasible tool in SQL databases that can be used to change the values already provided in the columns of the rows, or if a row is NULL (i.e., empty), this statement could be used to update that column of a row. The obvious example is the data we have used above. We shall now add data in property_type of id 001:

```
UPDATE apartments
SET
property_type = 'Luxury'
WHERE
      id = 001;
```

The statement above will add the string 'Luxury' in the property_type where the property's identification number is 001. You can change multiple columns of a row at a time by updating more values in the SET segment, and you can also add a condition under the WHERE statement. In that case, that column (or columns) will be updated in all rows that meet the given condition.

Select Query

When working with databases, the SELECT query is the primary focus of individuals when performing query optimization in many contexts. This is a complete game of fetching the data and making it available as soon as possible. Therefore, a sincere focus should be put upon the select statement. If required, you may select all data and display it, or you could select and display data that meets a particular condition (or a set of them). Moreover, you can also select just one record from the entire database, given that you have substantial information on it, preferably the id number that must always be unique. Example below:

```
SELECT * FROM apartments;
```

This is probably the simplest SELECT statement one can come across. It will simply fetch all the records in a given table and display them to the one that parsed this query. However, this is not the ideal practice in professional life because you do not need to fetch all the records. Moreover, databases at the scientific and corporate level usually have millions of records, which may take hours to fetch it entirely. Even if you fetch all the records, you cannot make sense of it (usually), and you will have a considerably hard time pinpointing the data you were originally looking for. Therefore, you have to usually restrict the number of columns (which could be in 1000s) and give certain conditions that will get you closer to the data you are looking for and save you a considerable amount of time and space. In those cases, however, the query may become complex.

You could also write the SELECT query like this:

```
SELECT id, rent, property_type
FROM   apartments
WHERE  id = 001;
```

This query will get you only the identification number, its rent, and the first property type. Assume that this table has millions of records by now; in this case, you have successfully fetched the exact record you were looking for amongst millions. However, it can get hard if you do not know the identification number since you will have to use queries in creative ways to get closer to your targeted property, but you may still not be able to reach the exact one (except in rare cases). Perhaps, you could narrow down a million records to a thousand or a few hundred of them.

Delete Query

The delete operation may be used if you want to remove records from a table. It has a very simple syntax, which is as follows:

```
DELETE FROM apartments
WHERE id = 001;
```

The statement above will delete the record from the table. If you delete a table, you remove it from the existence but only empty it (by removing all the records).

Truncate Query

The TRUNCATE statement is quite similar to the DELETE statement. You can use it to remove all the records from the table without removing the structure. Its execution is also quite simple, e.g., "TRUNCATE TABLE apartments;"

Drop Query

Unlike the DELETE and TRUNCATE statements, the DROP statement may be used to remove the database structure, along with all its records. In simpler terms, that would mean that the table will be removed from the database forever. In most cases you cannot retrieve the dropped data again; however, there are some ways of doing that. Nevertheless, its syntax is also quite simple:

```
DROP TABLE apartments;
```

Now, the apartments table has been removed from our hypothetical database, and so has the record (or potentially several records). In the case of an accident, the losses may be huge, but we can make a new table with the same name on the plus side, which is not possible if another table has the same name and is not dropped.

Chapter 2

Query Processing & Query Optimization

For anyone looking at the Query processing superficially, the name sounds quite self-explanatory. To put it in very basic terms, it is a process wherein a query is processed for execution. However, such a definition is quite simplistic and not enough. In fact, when you delve deeply into Query processing, you will see that it is actually quite complex and lengthy. That would be hard to fathom for the people new to Computer Science and Databases since these long processes are completed and executed in only a few seconds or a fraction of a second. The same goes for Query Processing. This term in itself is quite general, and this processing can be broken down into 4 main sub-components: decomposition, optimization, code generation, and program execution. From amongst all these things, the second one is the main focus of our book. As it is quite obvious, if you want to understand and delve into the subset of something, you first need to understand its superset, which is much more general and explanatory at a superficial level. It is important because understanding query processing will facilitate us in understanding query optimization. They cannot be independent of each other.

The Phases of Query Processing

Aforementioned, the reason query processing cannot be discussed separately is that its subcomponents are entire processes, each of which may require a book of its own if you need to understand it thoroughly (of which one is this one). We have broken down these phases sequentially, i.e., the process that comes first is discussed first and vice versa. By the end of this section, the need for optimization will also become apparent to you and establish a good ground for our discussions ahead.

Phase 1: Decomposition

This phase of query processing may also be called Query Parsing and Validation. This is a process wherein the code is decomposed or transformed to a more readable low-level language called relational algebra. Then, it is validated to see if the code is semantically and syntactically correct. The former means if the code makes sense or not, and the latter means if the code follows the right syntax that the grammar rules have set up.

This phase can be broken down into five fundamental parts:

1. **Analysis** – This is the most basic step of the first phase of query processing. The written code is verified lexically and syntactically to determine if all the basic language rules (i.e., syntax) are followed and if there is any mistake in the wording.

2. **Normalization** – If the query is deemed to be syntactically correct, it is moved to the second phase. Here the code is

converted into a normalized form so it can be manipulated much more easily. The two basic normalization forms are the Conjunctive Normal form and Disjunctive Normal form. This process is a technical one in itself, so its discussion is out of the scope of this book.

3. **Semantic Analysis** – This step determines if the query has any logical contradiction in it. The first step can determine if the syntax is correct, but it cannot logically work at the code. An example of a contradiction would be a SELECT query condition that asks for a product that has a price above $500 **AND** below $300 since both of them are not logically possible at the same time.

4. **Simplification** – Often, the written code can be in a form that is logically equivalent but considerably simple. This step aims to simplify it by removing redundant qualifications and common subexpressions. This may be considered an initial optimization of the query and will certainly be discussed ahead.

5. **Restructuring** – Now, the simplified query is restructured and then provided to the next stage, i.e., query optimization.

Phase 2: Query Optimization

Any query that the databased user gives can be executed in multiple ways if you give a good look at the relational algebra. However, means of execution may take considerably more time to execute, while others may be quite costly to the system. Therefore, there is a need to keep the balance between both. By that, by keeping both factors in mind, an execution method is chosen that will work considerably fast but will also not cost a lot. Since the fastest or cheapest method may be discarded at times, it can be called the middle-ground selection for execution. However, that doesn't mean the fastest or cheapest method cannot be chosen; at times, they can prove to be the most favorable choice in a given circumstance.

Once parsing is complete and the relational algebra has been provided, the optimizer calls all the relevant statistics about the data from the database and reaches a decision after deriving a conclusion from those statistics, i.e., the time that would be required to execute the given query, and its estimated cost. If we consider only the time, optimization becomes quite simple. However, as mentioned already, the fastest method may not always be in our best interest. More on query optimization will be discussed in this chapter and the remaining ones throughout this book.

Phase 3: Code Generation

The job of the optimizer is to determine the execution path that is to be followed. In this phase of query processing, the generator takes the scheduled plan as input from the optimizer. It uses its templates (i.e., holistic algorithms) to write out the plan that needs to be executed. In technical terms, these plans are called "access routines." There are several such routines, and all of them need to be written differently.

Phase 4: Execution of the Query

Finally, execution is the last stage of query processing. In a sense, it can be considered the very purpose of all the complex processes the database system had to go through in the above discussion. All the access routines that were written by the code generator will now the executed individually and sequentially, the result of which will be the complete execution of the query. By now, we are done with query processing.

Note that all of these complex processes were for a single query, which could be syntactically or semantically wrong. Every time the user gives a new query, the database goes through the entire processing phase until the query is executed or failed to execute due to technical faults in the query itself or some external factors (which are of no interest to us for now).

Fundamentals of Query Optimization

Now that we have discussed all the phases of query processing superficially, we shall move on to our next discussion: Query Optimization. Also note that starting this point, we are done with all the discussion surrounding but not directly related to optimization, so you will not be seeing more of them anymore, except perhaps, mere mentions of them for the sake of our discussions. However, we hope that our discussions above piqued your interest in the subject. If you want to read more on them, you can find a bunch of resources on them on Google, YouTube, or perhaps readily available textbooks and academic papers. Let's discuss the theory of Query Optimization in detail now.

Dynamic & Static Optimization

Regarding query optimization, there are two major approaches: (1) dynamic optimization and (2) static optimization. They are both commonly used in the industry, and each comes with its set of advantages and disadvantages.

In dynamic query optimization, both the parsing and optimization are carried out every time the user runs the query. This may prove beneficial to us if the statistics and certain components of the database have been updated, and a more efficient method of executing the given query may have emerged. However, on the downside, all these processes must run again every time, which could lead to a lag. Furthermore, one may have to limit the number of plans that need to be analyzed since frequent analysis can prove to be a problem. This may make you miss out on the best path for executing a given query in the database.

Then we have static query optimization. Contrary to dynamic query optimization, the parsing, validation, and optimization of a query are done only once. The run-time overhead (i.e., time taken to parse, validate and optimize again) is removed, allowing for analyzing a larger number of execution strategies compared to the dynamic optimization. This factor is especially good for queries that need to be run several times. On the downside, however, note that there is a chance that the optimal path which was found for a given query may not be optimal anymore, especially at the run-time. This could lead to a disaster potentially.

To make things better, however, most systems allow a hybrid approach to query optimization, wherein the database keeps an eye on if the statistics have changed drastically from the previous parsing and validation. If they have, these processes are repeated. If they have changed only a little, or not at all, then the static approach is used instead. It increases the efficiency even further.

Let's get into the subject at hand – SQL Query Optimization techniques.

Chapter 3

Query Optimization Techniques

If you want your application to succeed, you need to prevent problems from arising or, at the very least, fix any that do arise. Throughout the rest of this guide, we will go through several techniques in-depth, using different tools and practices to help you analyze performance issues and speed things up.

You could consider optimization as being akin to a good mystery story. The clues are all there – you just need to find them and follow them to the culprit. That's where we're going to start, learning how to identify the clues and use them to find the problems and fix them.

What is Optimization?
When you know the answer to that question, you will know when a problem is solved, and you can move on, looking for the next one. Queries can often be sped up, and there are different ways to do this, each with its own time and resource costs.

Developers cannot always spend the required resources to speed up their scripts, and, to be fair, they shouldn't want to. So, to keep it simple, we'll run with defining "optimal" as the point where a query has acceptable performance and keeps it for a decent amount of time.

If you have infinite resources – computing power, money, time, etc. – you can do pretty much anything, but few of us have that luxury and must define "done" whenever you need to deal with a performance issue.

With that, we have some useful checkpoints that will ensure we continually evaluate progress throughout the optimization. Those checkpoints are:

1. The query is performing adequately.

2. Further optimization is too expensive in terms of resources.

3. We've got to the point of diminishing returns, and there is little point in going on.

4. We discover another solution that means our current optimization is no longer needed.

Many people think that over-optimization is better than under but, it's a waste as far as resources go. Let's say we have a huge covering index that really isn't necessary. Whenever a table is written to for a long time, the computing resources needed are eye-watering. If you have to rewrite a previously acceptable code, it costs in terms of development time and QA time. And if you try to tweak a query that is already working well, you may gain a small amount of optimization, but the resource cost isn't worth it.

In SQL Query Optimization, you have one goal - solve your problem adequately; don't try to over-solve it.

What a Query Does

These are the questions that need answering:

- What is the purpose of the query?
- What should the results look like?
- What kind of UI, report, or code is the query being generated by?

It's common for us to want to dive right in and fight the problem as quickly as possible. We get traces running, execution plans in place, and we collect timing and IO statistics before we suddenly realize we don't really have a clue.

The first step is to stand back. Understand your query and ask yourself these questions to help with the optimization:

- **What size is the result set?** Do we need to be prepared for a few rows or millions returned?

- **Do any parameters have limited values?** Will a parameter have the same value all the time? Are there limitations on any value that can simplify things for us and remove one or more research avenues?

- **How often will the query be executed?** If it runs once a day, it will not be treated the same as one that runs every second, for example.

- **Do any unusual or invalid values indicate a problem with the application?** Have you set an input to NULL, and it shouldn't be? Have any other inputs be set to values that don't make any sense, are contradictory, or don't fit the query's use case?

- **How often is the query executed?** Something that occurs once a day will be treated very differently than one that is run every second.

- **Are there any invalid or unusual input values that are indicative of an application problem?** Is one input set to NULL, but never should be NULL? Are any other inputs set to values that make no sense, are contradictory, or otherwise go against the use-case of the query?

- **Can you see any obvious optimization, syntactical, or logical problems?** Can you see anything off the bat that will cause a problem, regardless of variables, such as parameter values?

- **What do you consider acceptable performance for a query?** How fast should it be? How much reduction in resource consumption is needed to improve server performance? How is the query performing now? That last question is your starting point, so you know what improvement is required.

If you ask these questions before you optimize the query, you eliminate the risk of a situation where hours are wasted in collecting query data, only to find you don't understand how to use it.

The results from this can often provide better solutions. Perhaps you don't need that new index, after all, or maybe that large query could be broken down into several smaller ones. Perhaps one of the parameter values is wrong, or UI or code problem needs resolving. You get the picture.

The Tools

Let's keep things simple here and use just a few tools.

Execution Plans

These provide graphical representations, showing the optimizer's decision-making process in executing a query. Note that an entire chapter is dedicated to these later, so don't worry if you don't understand them now.

In the execution plan, we can see the tables that were accessed and how. We can see how they were joined and all other operations that happened. That includes the query costs, which are estimated values for a query component's overall expense. It also includes tons of data, such as I/O cost, row size, CPU cost, and details on the utilized indexes.

Generally, we want to find scenarios where a given operation in the plan is processing large numbers of rows. When we find a high-cost component, we can delve into what's caused it and how we can fix it.

STATISTICS IO

This tool lets us see the number of physical and logical reads made when queries are executed. It can be interactively turned on in SQL Server Management Studio (SSMS) with the TSQL below:

SET STATISTICS IO ON;

Switch it on, and you will see the Messages pane showing you extra data, including the ProductModel, Scan count, and the logical and physical reads.

The logical read count indicates the number of reads from the buffer cache, and that number is what we refer to when we talk of the read the query is responsible for or the level of IO it causes.

Physical reads indicate the data read from storage devices – this is data not available in present memory. If you see that data is constantly being read from storage devices and not memory, it's a good indication of memory capacity or buffer cache issues.

Typically, the main cause of bottlenecks and latency in slow queries is IO. The STATISTICS IO unit of measurement is:

STATISTICS IO = 1 read = on 8KB page = 8192 bytes

Query Duration

The top reason for needing to research a slow query is that a user has complained of its speed – or lack of. Often, the time a query takes to execute is the biggest indicator of an issue with performance.

We will manually measure the duration for our purposes and, if you look at the bottom corner of SSMS, you can see that timer.

You can use other methods to measure the query duration accurately, including setting STATISTICS TIME. However, we will only look at slow enough queries to not need that level of accuracy. It's easy to see when a query that takes 30 seconds is quicker to run in a sub-second time, reinforcing the user's role as a great feedback source in speeding up applications.

Your Eyes

A high percentage of performance issues arise from the query patterns we'll be discussing shortly. Pattern recognition lets us eliminate vast amounts of research because we can see, at a glance, that something isn't written right.

The more queries we optimize, the easier and quicker it becomes to identify these patterns and indicators, and we will know that these issues can be fixed quickly without wasting time on research.

We'll also be looking for logic hints that tell us if there are any issues with the application, or parameters, or flaws in the query generation that may need others to get involved in fixing it.

What the Query Optimizer Does

All queries run on the same basic TSQL process to execute on SQL servers:

- **Parsing** – This process checks the query syntax, looking to see if the TSQL rules are being followed and the keywords are valid. You will get error messages at this point if you forgot to add a semicolon before a table expression, spelled something wrong, used a reserved keyword to name a column, and so on.

- **Binding** – This process checks the object references in the TSQL against defined temporary objects and the system catalogs to see if they are valid and correctly referenced. It retrieves information about the objects, like the constraints, data types, or whether columns show NULL. This results in a query tree comprised of a list showing the processes required for the query to execute. However, this is only a basic list, and there are no specifics at this stage, such as which joins or indexes should be used.

- **Optimization** – This is the process we will be talking about the most. The optimizer works in much the same way as a gaming computer. It must consider a vast number of moves in a very short time, eliminate the bad choice, so it's left with the best possible one. There could be millions of combinations for the optimizer to consider at any time, and only a small handful will make it through. If you have played chess against a computer, you will know that it is more likely to make mistakes if it has less time to move.

Instead of chess moves, we'll be talking about execution plans which, as you know, are the steps the execution engine follows in processing a query. A query will have multiple choices to make to get to that plan and only a short time to do it in.

The choices will include these questions:

- In what order should the tables be joined?
- Which joins do we need for the tables?
- Which indexes are required?
- Does a given table require a seek and scan?
- Which offers more benefit - caching the data in worktables or spooling it for use in the future?

The optimizer's execution plans must all return the same results, but each may differ in performance, primarily due to the above questions, along with others.

Query optimization is incredibly CPU-intensive. It requires a lot of computing resources to go through plans, and finding the right one may take more time than there is available. This means a balance must be achieved and maintained between the required resources for optimization, execution and the time needed for the entire process to finish. Therefore, the optimizer isn't designed to choose the best plan but to find the best one after a given time period has passed. It may be perfect, but that is a limitation of a process with too many possibilities to consider.

The metric that judges the plans and decides which should be considered is called a query cost. It doesn't have a unit and is a relative measure of the required resources for each execution plan step. The overall cost is the cost of each step summed, and these can be seen in any execution plan. They include the estimated operator cost, IO cost, CPU cost, and subtree cost.

Each query's subtree costs are calculated and will be used for one of these:

- To remove an execution plan with a high cost attached, along with similar ones, from all the available plans

- Rank the execution plans left in the pool based on their cost.

The query cost may be useful in helping you understand how a query has been optimized, but you must remember that its main role is to help the optimizer choose the best plans. It doesn't give you a direct measure of CPU, IO, duration, memory, or any other important metric to a user waiting for the query to execute.

If you get a low query cost, don't assume it means the best plan or a fast query. Conversely, high costs are not always bad. As such, a heavy reliance on query cost as a performance metric is not recommended.

As the optimizer goes through the plans, it puts them in order from highest cost to lowest and, eventually, it will come to one of these conclusions:

- All the plans have been looked at, and the best chosen

- There's not enough time to go through them all, and the best one looked at to now is chosen.

Once the plan is chosen, the optimizer has finished, and we can go to the final processing step.

- **Execution** – This is the last step where the SQL server takes the identified execution plan and follows the instructions to execute the query.

Note

Optimization is very expensive so, SQL Server has an execution plan cache. Here, details are stored about all queries executed on a server and which plan was used. Most databases run the same queries repeatedly, like social media posts, web searches, and so on. Plan reuse makes it easier and cheaper to optimize some queries because the work is already done.

Common Query Optimization Themes

Let's get into the topic of optimization. The list below details the common metrics you can use to help you optimize a query. These processes can identify patterns, tips, and tricks in the query structure that may indicate performance is below par.

Index Scans

You can access data from indexes using a scan or seek. The latter is a specified selection of rows based on a narrow filter—the former searches all the indexes to return the required data. If there are a million rows in the table, the scan would need to go through all of them, while a seek of that table would quickly go through the binary tree to return the required data.

If you need a large amount of data returned, an index scan is probably the best option. For example, if you needed 950,000 rows from your 1 million row table, the index scan would do much better, while a seek would be best if you only wanted 20 rows.

You can spot an index scan in an execution plan very easily:

```
SELECT
            *
FROM Sales.OrderTracking
INNER JOIN Sales.SalesOrderHeader
ON SalesOrderHeader.SalesOrderID =
OrderTracking.SalesOrderID
INNER JOIN Sales.SalesOrderDetail
ON SalesOrderDetail.SalesOrderID =
SalesOrderHeader.SalesOrderID
WHERE OrderTracking.EventDateTime = '2021-
05-29 00:00:00';
```

The resulting execution plan would show the index scan in the top corner. In our case, it would show that 90% of the query's resources were consumed, and the index scan is labeled as clustered. STATISTICS IO also shows the OrderTracking table to have a significant number of reads against it.

When an undesired scan is identified, there are several solutions. When you resolve index scan issues, you should consider the following:

- Is there an available index to handle the query's filter?

- If not, should one be created to improve the query's performance? Does the query get executed enough to warrant this? Be aware that indexes improve read speed performance but reduce write speed, so they should be used cautiously.

- Is there an index?

- Is the filter valid? Is the column one that should never be filtered on?

- Is the index scan being caused by another query pattern that we can resolve? We'll talk about this a bit more shortly.

- Is this a query for which a scan cannot be avoided?

- Is the query one for which there is no way to avoid a scan? Some query filters must search the whole table because they are all-inclusive.

Joins and WHERE Clauses Wrapped in Functions

Optimization constantly focuses on the WHERE clause and joins. Because IO is usually the most expensive, and these two components can significantly limit it, this is where the worst performance offenders are usually found. The faster the data can be sliced down to just the required rows, the more efficient the execution.

When a WHERE clause is evaluated, all involved expressions must be resolved before the data is returned. If there are functions around a column, like SUBSTRING, CONVERT, or DATEPART, they must also be resolved. Should the function require evaluating to determine the result before execution, the entire data set must be scanned.

Have a look at this query:

```
SELECT
      Person.BusinessEntityID,
      Person.FirstName,
      Person.LastName,
      Person.MiddleName
FROM Person.Person
WHERE LEFT(Person.LastName, 3) = 'For';
```

The result set will contain rows from Person.Person with the last name starting in "For."

Although just four rows are returned, the whole index was scanned to get those rows. Why? Because Person.Person contains a LEFT join. Logically, the query is right and will return the data we expect, but SQL Server must evaluate LEFT against every row to see which ones fit the filter. This will force an index scan, but this can be avoided.

When a WHERE clause or a join has functions, consider how the function could be moved to the scalar variable. Also, consider how the query could be rewritten to leave the table columns clean, i.e., without any functions.

We can rewrite the query above to do that:

```
SELECT
      Person.BusinessEntityID,
      Person.FirstName,
      Person.LastName,
      Person.MiddleName
FROM Person.Person
WHERE Person.LastName LIKE 'For%';
```

Here, we used LIKE, and we moved the wildcard logic to the string literal. This cleaned the LastName column, allowing the SQL Server to seek the indexes against the column.

The query tweak we made was relatively minor, but it gave the optimizer the chance to use the index seek, pulling the required data – and it only took two reads, not 117 this time.

This technique is all about ensuring the columns are clean. So, when you write your queries, don't hesitate to put your complex numeric, data, or string logic on the scalar variables or parameters rather than on the columns. If you are trying to find the issue with a poor performer and spot that column names are wrapped in user-defined or system functions, start thinking about how to push the functions into other scalar sections of the query. Doing that allows

SQL Server to seek indexes instead of scanning, resulting in a more efficient decision for the query execution.

Implicit Conversions

As you saw in the last section, when functions are wrapped around columns, the result is poor query performance, unintentional table scans, and increased latency. Implicit conversions behave much the same, but they are not in plain sight.

SQL Server must reconcile data types when it compares values. These data types are all given precedence in SQL, and the one with the lowest precedence is converted to the higher precedence data type automatically.

Some conversions are seamless and don't have any impact on performance. For example, you can compare a VARCHAR(MAX) and a VARCHAR(50) with no problems. Similarly, you can compare BIGINT and TINYINT, DATETIME and TIME, or TIME with a VARCHAR representation of one of the TIME types. However, you cannot automatically compare all data types.

We've filtered the SELECT query below against an indexed column:

```
SELECT
    EMP.BusinessEntityID,
    EMP.LoginID,
    EMP.JobTitle
FROM HumanResources.Employee EMP
WHERE EMP.NationalIDNumber = 658797903;
```

It would be easy to assume that this results in an index seek and the query efficiently returning the data.

However, although we only wanted one row against that indexed column, we ended up with a full table scan. So, what happened? If you were to examine the execution plan for this, you would see a big hint in the form of a yellow exclamation mark on the SELECT operation.

If you hover the mouse over the operator, you can see a warning – CONVERT_IMPLICIT. When you see one of these, it indicates that you are trying to compare data types that are sufficiently different that they cannot be converted. So, SQL Server will convert all the table values before the filter is applied.

If you were to hover the mouse over the SSMS NationalIDNumber column, you would see confirmation that it's an NVARCHAR(15), which you are trying to compare with a numeric value. There is an easy solution, similar to having functions on columns – the conversion needs to be moved off the column to the scalar value. In our case, the scalar value of 658797903 is changed to a string representation of '658797903':

```
SELECT
    EMP.BusinessEntityID,
    EMP.LoginID,
    EMP.JobTitle
FROM HumanResources.Employee EMP
WHERE EMP.NationalIDNumber = '658797903'
```

This is a very simple change, and it changes how the optimizer handles the query, resulting in an index seek, less IO, and no implicit conversion warning.

You can spot implicit conversion warnings easily because the SQL Server will give you a big warning in the execution plan. Once you spot the problem, check the column's data types and resolve it.

In the next chapter, we'll look at some ore query optimization tips and tricks.

Chapter 4

Query Optimization Tips and Tricks

If you need to fix poor performance issues or bad queries, it can take hours, sometimes days, of constant researching and testing. However, if you can learn to identify some common design patterns that indicate poor performance, you can cut that time significantly.

Learning pattern recognition allows you to spot the easy issues quickly, leaving you free to focus on what caused the problem. Conversely, performance tuning can take hours because extended events must be collected, along with execution plans, traces, and statistics. Because of that, early identification of potential issues can eliminate much of the work.

While due diligence must be performed to prove that your changes are optimal, one of the biggest time-savers is knowing where to start.

Tips and Tricks

To that end, we're going to look at some tips and tricks that can help speed up your query optimization time.

The WHERE Clause in Several Columns/The OR Clause in the Join Predicate

SQL Server can filter data sets quite efficiently with indexes. These are used via the WHERE clause or through a combination of filters separated with an AND operator. Because they are exclusive, the operations can take the date and slice it, cutting it into progressively smaller chunks until all that remains is the result set.

The OR clause is quite a different tale. This operator is inclusive, meaning it cannot be processed in one operation by the SQL Server. Rather, each OR component has to be independently evaluated. This is quite an expensive operation, but the results can be concatenated and returned normally.

One scenario where the OR clause will perform very poorly is when several tables or columns are involved. Not only does each OR component need to be evaluated, but that path must be followed through all other query tables and filters.

Below you can see an example of OR causing more trouble than you thought possible:

```
SELECT DISTINCT
    PRODUCT.ProductID,
    PRODUCT.Name
FROM Production.Product PRODUCT
INNER JOIN Sales.SalesOrderDetail DETAIL
ON PRODUCT.ProductID = DETAIL.ProductID
OR PRODUCT.rowguid = DETAIL.rowguid;
```

This is a simple query. It has two tables and one join responsible for checking rowguid and ProductID. It doesn't matter if neither table was indexed; we still expect a table scan on both SaleOrderDetails and Product. It may be expensive, but we can understand it.

Both tables were scanned but what took an inordinate amount of computing power was processing OR – over a million reads! That is a lot considering there are only 504 rows in Product and 121317 rows in SalesOrderDetail – we ended up reading way more data than both tables contained. Plus, it took a lot longer to execute and that was on a high-powered computer.

This is quite scary, but we can learn one thing from it – SQL Server struggles to process OR conditions where multiple columns are involved. Perhaps the best way to deal with this is to eliminate the OR condition where possible or break it down into several smaller queries. It may not be the most elegant solution to break short queries down into a more drawn out one, but it may be the best choice when faced with OR issues:

```
SELECT
      PRODUCT.ProductID,
      PRODUCT.Name
FROM Production.Product PRODUCT
INNER JOIN Sales.SalesOrderDetail DETAIL
ON PRODUCT.ProductID = DETAIL.ProductID
UNION
SELECT
      PRODUCT.ProductID,
      PRODUCT.Name
FROM Production.Product PRODUCT
INNER JOIN Sales.SalesOrderDetail DETAIL
```

```
ON PRODUCT.rowguid = DETAIL.rowguid
```

In this rewritten query, each OR component was transformed into a SELECT statement. The result set is concatenated with UNION, and the duplicates are removed.

However, the execution plan is more complex because each table is now being queried twice rather than once. We cut the reads down to just 750, and the execution was at least twice as fast as before.

You will see that the execution plan still shows loads of index scans, but we still have far better performance, even though the tables are being scanned four times.

When you include an OR clause in a query, be cautious. Test the performance, verify its adequacy and ensure you don't introduce something similar to the example above by accident. Should you be reviewing an application that isn't performing well, and you see an OR over different tables or columns, focus on that as your potential problem – it's an easy query pattern to identify, and it nearly always results in poor performance.

Wildcard String Searches

Searching strings efficiently is somewhat challenging, and there are more inefficient ways to do it than efficient. For string columns that are searched frequently, we must ensure the following:

- The searched columns have indexes

- They are usable indexes

- If not, can full-text indexes be used?

- If not, can n-grams, hashes, or another solution be used?

If you don't add design considerations or extra features, SQL Server isn't very efficient at searching strings. For example, if we wanted to see if a string were present at any column position, it would be quite inefficient to retrieve that data:

```
SELECT
        Person.BusinessEntityID,
        Person.FirstName,
        Person.LastName,
        Person.MiddleName
FROM Person.Person
WHERE Person.LastName LIKE '%For%';
```

Here, we are looking at LastName to see if there are any instances of "For" in the string. When we used a % at the start of a string, it is to ensure we make it impossible to use any ascending index. Conversely, when the % is at the end, it is impossible to use any descending index.

As we would expect, the result is Person.Person being scanned. There is only one way to learn if a text column contains a specified substring – every character must be gone through in every row in a search to find every occurrence of the string. This works okay on small tables, but it will be painfully slow where you have massive data sets!

We can go at this situation in a few ways:

1. The application could be re-evaluated. Does a wildcard search need to be done in this manner? Does anyone really want to search entire columns looking for a specific string? If you can answer no to both, remove the capability – problem gone.

2. Can we reduce the data size by applying other filters to the query before the string comparison is done? Perhaps we could filter by a common criteria, such as status, time, or date, to help us reduce the data that needs scanning to a more manageable size.

3. Can a leading string search be done rather than the wildcard search? For example, could we replace %For% with For%?

4. Is it possible to do full-text indexing? If it is available, can it be implemented and used?

5. Can an n-gram or query hash solution?

Options one through three are not just optimization solutions. They are also design or architecture considerations, and they are asking what we can assume, understand or change about the query so it can be tweaked to work efficiently. All of these need you to understand or be able to change the data the query returns.

While these options may not always be available to you, all parties need to be on the same page as far as string searches go. Let's say you have a table with a billion rows, and frequent searches for strings in any position in an NVARCHAR(MAX) column are done. In that case, discussions are needed between involved parties regarding why this is happening and if alternatives are available. Suppose it is crucial to have that functionality. In that case, more resources need to be committed to supporting string searching – it is an expensive function – or you must accept serious latency and high resource consumption.

One useful SQL Server feature is Full-Text Indexing. Indexes are generated to provide the capability of flexible string searches on any text column, including wildcard searches and linguistic searching. The latter uses a given language's rules to make the right decisions on whether phrases or words have enough similarity to a column's contents to be a match. While Full-Text is relatively flexible, it does need installing, configuring, and maintaining. However, where an application is string-centric, it is the perfect solution.

Another option that works well for short string columns is the n-gram. These are string segments, and we can store them away from the data we want to search. They provide substring searching ability without having to scan large tables. Before we dive into this, there are some things you need to understand, in particular, the search rules an application uses:

- Does a search allow for a minimum or a maximum number of characters?

- Are tables cans/empty searches allowed?

- Are phrases or multiple words allowed?

- Do substrings need to be stored at the start of the string? If required, an index seek can be used to collect these.

When these considerations have been assessed, a string column can be broken down into string segments. For example, take a string search with a three-character minimum search length, looking for the word "Dinosaur." The three-character or longer substrings of that word are as follows. Note that the beginning of the string is ignored. This is because an index seek can be used against the column to gather that quickly:

- ino

- inos

- inosa

- inosau

- inosaur

- nos

- nosa

- nosau

- nosaur

- osa

- osau

- osaur

- sau

- saur

- aur.

These are known as n-grams, and if we created another table to store each substring, we could link them to the row in the large table with "Dinosaur" in it. Rather than scanning a huge table, we simply run an equality search on the n-gram table. Let's say we wanted to do a wildcard search for "dino" – we can redirect that search on one that looks like this:

```
SELECT
       n_gram_table.my_big_table_id_column
FROM dbo.n_gram_table
WHERE n_gram_table.n_gram_data = 'Dino';
```

If n_gram_data has been indexed, all IDs with the word "Dino" anywhere in them will be returned quickly. The n-gram table requires just two columns, and the n-gram string size can be bound using the application rules from above. Even if the table expanded rapidly, we would still likely get very fast searches.

This approach's main cost is maintenance. The n-gram table must be updated whenever we insert or delete a row or update the string data. And, as the column size grows, so too will the number of n-grams in each row. This is a great solution for short strings, such as phone numbers, names, or zip codes but is costly for longer strings, such as descriptions, email text, and other MAX-length columns.

Large Write Operations

Let's look at a scenario where iteration can significantly improve performance. Contention is one optimization component we haven't yet discussed. When operations are performed against data, locks are taken against some data, ensuring consistent results that don't get in the way of other queries the data may be executing at the same time.

Locking and blocking are both good at safeguarding data from being corrupted and providing protection against bad results. However, if contention continues for some time, we may find critical queries have to wait, and that causes latency and makes users unhappy.

The larger write operations are the epitome of contention because, often, in the time taken to update data and indexes, check the constraints, and process any triggers, they can lock the whole table up. So, how large is too large? Well, there are no real rules. If your table has no foreign keys or triggers, it could be anywhere from 50,000 to a million rows, while, on a table with lots of triggers and constraints, it could be as low as 2000. There is only one way to confirm the problem – test, observe, and respond as required.

Large write operations also generate a high level of log file growth. When large volumes of data are being written, you must monitor the transaction log and ensure it doesn't get filled up or, worse, the physical storage location doesn't get filled up.

Often, these large operations are a result of your own work, including load processes for data warehousing, software releases, ETL processes, and other operations that require large amounts of data written, even if not very often. We need to identify how much contention is allowed in the tables before those processes are run. If a large table were loaded during a maintenance window while it wasn't in use by anyone else, we could deploy the strategy we want. On the other hand, if we were writing to a busy production site, the best way to safeguard against contention would be to reduce how many rows are modified in each operation.

Some of the more common operations resulting in large write operations are:

- Adding new columns to tables and backfilling them across the whole table

- Updating columns across the whole table

- Changing a column's data type

- Importing large amounts of new data

- Deleting or archiving large amounts of old data

Often, this may not even cause performance issues, but it is important to understand how large write operations can affect things. That way, you can avoid many related issues, such as maintenance events or releases going awry.

Missing Indexes

Whether through execution plan XML, Management Studio GUI, or a missing index DMV, SQL Server will tell us about missing indexes that could affect query performance.

This is a useful warning because it tells us that we can improve query performance with a relatively painless fix. On the other hand, it is misleading because latency issues aren't always best fixed with an extra index. Although we are given details about a new index, there is some work we need to do before taking the advice of the Server. We need to know:

- Are there any similar existing indexes that we could modify to cover this?

- Are all of the include columns needed, or could we get away with only using an index on the sorting columns?

- Is the index impact high? How high? Will it provide a 5% or 95% improvement to the query?

- Is this index already in existence but not being chosen by the query optimizer?

Often, the indexes suggested by SQL Server are excessive. Here's an example of the statement creating the index for the previously discussed partial plan:

```
CREATE NONCLUSTERED INDEX <Name of Missing
Index, sysname,>
ON Sales.SalesOrderHeader
(Status,SalesPersonID)
INCLUDE (SalesOrderID,SubTotal)
```

Look at the result from this.

Here, we have an index already on SalesPersonID. Status is a table column that usually contains a single value. This means it won't give us much value as a sorting column. 19% isn't too impressive an impact, and it would leave us asking if the query was important enough to do this. If the query were executed a million or more times per day, then the work may well be worth it but, if it is only executed a few times, it probably isn't.

In that case, we could consider a different index recommendation in which the suggested missing index is:

```
CREATE NONCLUSTERED INDEX [<Name of Missing
Index, sysname,>]
ON [Person].[Person] ([FirstName])
INCLUDE ([BusinessEntityID],[Title])
```

We would get a 93% improvement from the suggested index this time, and the unindexed column called FirstName would be handled. In the event this query is run frequently, the addition of this index is a good move.

59

A more subjective question would be, do we need to Title and BusinessEntityID as INCLUDE columns? In this case, we need to know if our query is critical enough that we don't ever want a key lookup to get the additional columns from the clustered index. This goes back to one of our first questions – how do we know we have the optimal query performance? Should the non-covering index be sufficient, the right decision would be to stop there as we could avoid using extra resources unnecessarily. But, if the performance still isn't up to par, the logical thing to do is add in the INCLUDE columns.

The important thing to remember is that indexes need to be maintained, and write operations need to be slowed down. Once we understand that, we can take a pragmatic approach to indexing to avoid the following mistakes:

- **We over-index tables** – too many indexes in a table slow down the write operations with every UPDATE, INSERT, and DELETE operation on an indexed column – this is because the indexes are constantly updating. The indexes also take extra space in database backups and storage.

- **We under-index tables** – tables with too few indexes are not effective at serving read queries. In an ideal world, the common queries that get executed against tables should gain some benefit from the indexes. Those queries executed less frequently are evaluated on a per-case requirement and indexed when it is best to do so. If you are trying to find the cause of a performance issue on a table with few nonclustered indexes, the most likely cause is under-indexing. In this case, add indexes as needed.

- **There is no primary key or clustered index** – every table should have both. A clustered index performs much better than a heap on almost every occasion, giving us the infrastructure we need to include non-clustered indexes efficiently when we need them. Primary keys provide the query optimizer with valuable information to help it make the right decisions in the execution plans it creates. If a table has only one or neither of these, you will know where to look to start resolving the performance issues.

High Table Count

The query optimizer will face similar challenges to any relational query optimizer – it must find the best execution plan, in the shortest time, despite having many options to consider. Essentially, it is constantly evaluating, throwing away plans that match or nearly match the suboptimal one, and setting aside potential candidates. This is much like a computer playing chess, evaluating every move. The more tables a query has, the bigger the chessboard and, with many more options, SQL has to work that much harder in the same short time span.

As new tables are added to a query, its complexity will increase. Typically, an optimizer will make good decisions, even with so many tables. However, by adding new tables, we significantly increase the risk of getting an inefficient plan. I'm not saying that queries with lots of tables are bad. What I'm saying is that caution is needed when you increase a query's size. The optimizer needs to work out the join order and type for each set of tables and how and when aggregation and filters should be applied.

Based on the join used, queries fall into one of these basic forms:

- **Left-Deep Tree** – A joins B, B joins C, and so on. In this query, tables are joined sequentially, one after the other.

- **Bushy Tree** – A joins B, A joins C, B joins D, and so on. In this query, the tables are branched into several logical units in each tree branch.

This is what a bushy tree looks like:

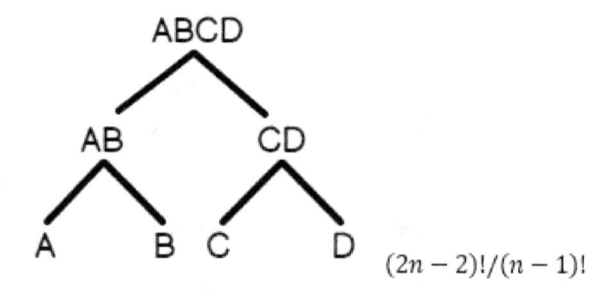

```
        ABCD
        /  \
      AB    CD
      /\    /\
     A  B  C  D
```
$(2n-2)!/(n-1)!$

While a deep-left tree looks like this:

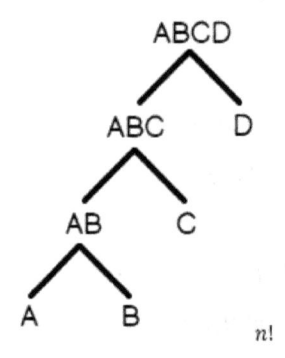

```
         ABCD
         /  \
       ABC   D
       / \
      AB  C
      /\
     A  B
```
$n!$

The left-deep tree has a more natural order, based on how the tables join, which means there are far fewer suitable execution plans than with the bushy tree. You can see the mathematics behind all this on each image, working out the number of plans generated, on average, for a query type.

Given that mathematics is critical, here's an example to show you how it works. This query has access to 12 tables:

```
SELECT TOP 25
      Product.ProductID,
      Product.Name AS ProductName,
      Product.ProductNumber,
      CostMeasure.UnitMeasureCode,
      CostMeasure.Name AS CostMeasureName,
      ProductVendor.AverageLeadTime,
      ProductVendor.StandardPrice,
      ProductReview.ReviewerName,
      ProductReview.Rating,
      ProductCategory.Name AS CategoryName,
      ProductSubCategory.Name AS
SubCategoryName
FROM Production.Product
INNER JOIN Production.ProductSubCategory
ON ProductSubCategory.ProductSubcategoryID =
Product.ProductSubcategoryID
INNER JOIN Production.ProductCategory
ON ProductCategory.ProductCategoryID =
ProductSubCategory.ProductCategoryID
INNER JOIN Production.UnitMeasure
SizeUnitMeasureCode
ON Product.SizeUnitMeasureCode =
SizeUnitMeasureCode.UnitMeasureCode
INNER JOIN Production.UnitMeasure
WeightUnitMeasureCode
```

```
ON Product.WeightUnitMeasureCode =
WeightUnitMeasureCode.UnitMeasureCode
INNER JOIN Production.ProductModel
ON ProductModel.ProductModelID =
Product.ProductModelID
LEFT JOIN
Production.ProductModelIllustration
ON ProductModel.ProductModelID =
ProductModelIllustration.ProductModelID
LEFT JOIN
Production.ProductModelProductDescriptionCul
ture
ON
ProductModelProductDescriptionCulture.Produc
tModelID = ProductModel.ProductModelID
LEFT JOIN Production.ProductDescription
ON ProductDescription.ProductDescriptionID =
ProductModelProductDescriptionCulture.Produc
tDescriptionID
LEFT JOIN Production.ProductReview
ON ProductReview.ProductID =
Product.ProductID
LEFT JOIN Purchasing.ProductVendor
ON ProductVendor.ProductID =
Product.ProductID
LEFT JOIN Production.UnitMeasure CostMeasure
ON ProductVendor.UnitMeasureCode =
CostMeasure.UnitMeasureCode
ORDER BY Product.ProductID DESC;
```

This is a relatively busy query and, with 12 tables, the match would be:

(2n-2)! / (n-1)! = (2*12-1)! / (12-1)! = 28,158,588,057,600 possible execution plans.

If we had a more linear query, it would be:

n! = 12! = 479,001,600 possible execution plans.

Now, that is just for 12 tables. Imagine if your query had many more, say 50 0r 100 tables. While the optimizer may be able to slice the numbers quickly by removing tons of sub-optimal options, but the odds decrease of getting a decent plan the more tables are added.

Some of the more useful methods to optimizing queries with a large number of queries include:

- Move the lookup tables or metadata to another query, where the data is placed into a temporary table.

- Move joins for returning single constants into parameters or variables.

- Break larger queries into many smaller ones, with data sets that can be joined when you are ready.

- If your query is heavily used, think about an indexed view to help streamline the need for constant access to critical data.

- Remove joins, subqueries, and unneeded tables.

When you break a query down into smaller ones, you need to ensure that any data change between them will not invalidate the result. If your query must be an atomic set, you will probably need to use a combination of transactions, isolation levels, and locking to maintain data integrity.

Mostly, when you join many tables, the query may be broken into small logical units you can execute separately. For our earlier example using 12 tables, unused ones could be removed, and the data retrieval split into two queries:

```
SELECT TOP 25
       Product.ProductID,
       Product.Name AS ProductName,
       Product.ProductNumber,
       ProductCategory.Name AS
ProductCategory,
       ProductSubCategory.Name AS
ProductSubCategory,
       Product.ProductModelID
INTO #Product
FROM Production.Product
INNER JOIN Production.ProductSubCategory
ON ProductSubCategory.ProductSubcategoryID =
Product.ProductSubcategoryID
INNER JOIN Production.ProductCategory
ON ProductCategory.ProductCategoryID =
ProductSubCategory.ProductCategoryID
ORDER BY Product.ModifiedDate DESC;

SELECT
       Product.ProductID,
       Product.ProductName,
       Product.ProductNumber,
       CostMeasure.UnitMeasureCode,
       CostMeasure.Name AS CostMeasureName,
       ProductVendor.AverageLeadTime,
       ProductVendor.StandardPrice,
```

```
            ProductReview.ReviewerName,
            ProductReview.Rating,
            Product.ProductCategory,
            Product.ProductSubCategory
FROM #Product Product
INNER JOIN Production.ProductModel
ON ProductModel.ProductModelID =
Product.ProductModelID
LEFT JOIN Production.ProductReview
ON ProductReview.ProductID =
Product.ProductID
LEFT JOIN Purchasing.ProductVendor
ON ProductVendor.ProductID =
Product.ProductID
LEFT JOIN Production.UnitMeasure CostMeasure
ON ProductVendor.UnitMeasureCode =
CostMeasure.UnitMeasureCode;

DROP TABLE #Product;
```

This is just one potential solution and can help reduce complex queries into smaller ones. It also allows us to review the tables and eliminates any that we don't needs, along with unneeded variables, columns, or anything else that isn't required.

Table count contributes significantly to bad execution plans because it forces the optimizer to look through a much bigger result set, potentially discarding valid results to keep the search quick. If your query is performing badly and has many tables, split it down into small ones. While it may not give a great improvement, it can be effective when all else has failed, and you have lots of tables constantly being read in one query.

Query Hints

Query hints are explicit directions given to the query optimizer. In giving this instruction, we bypass the optimizer's rules to force it to behave how it normally wouldn't. In this way, it is less of a hint and more of a directive.

We often use query hints when we have performance issues, and hints can sometimes fix the issues. For example, SQL Server provides plenty of hints that affect join types, isolation levels, table locking, and much more. However, while they may be good for some things, they do present a risk to performance for the following reasons:

- Changes made to the schema or data in the future may mean a hint no longer applies and, until it is removed, it just gets in the way.

- Hints can hide major problems, like huge data requests, missing indexes, or business logic that doesn't work as it should. However, it is always more preferable to solve the root cause than a symptom.

- Hints can cause strange behavior, like bad data coming from dirty reads through NOLOCK.

- When a hint is applied to an edge case, it may degrade the performance for other scenarios.

Generally, query hints should not be applied too often. They should only be applied once enough research has been done, and when you know for definite, it won't cause any bad changes.

Some notes to remember on the commonly used hints are:

- **NOLOCK** – Should data be locked, the SQL Server knows to read the data from the last available value we know of – this is called a dirty read. Because a mixture of old and new values can be used, there may be inconsistencies in the data sets. As such, NOLOCK should never be used where data quality is critical.

- **RECOMPILE** – When this is added to the end of a query, a new execution plan is generated whenever the query is executed. So, RECOMPILE shouldn't be used on any queries that are executed a lot as the cost is somewhat expensive. It is effective at avoiding unnecessary plan reuse on infrequent processes or reports, though. Often, RECOMPILE is used as a kind of sticking plaster when we have out of date statistics or parameter sniffing is happening,

- **MERGE/HASH/LOOP** – This lets the query optimizer know that a particular join should be used for a join operation. However, this is high-risk because the best join changes as the parameters, schema, and data change over time. So, while it can fix an immediate problem, it does bring in a certain amount of technical debt that stays all the while the hint is there.

- **OPTIMIZE FOR** – This specifies parameter values that the query should be optimized for. Often, it is used when we need to control performance for common use cases to stop outliers messing up the plan cache. However, this is quite fragile and may become unusable once business logic has changed.

Let's go back to the search query we did earlier:

```
SELECT
   e.BusinessEntityID,
   p.Title,
   p.FirstName,
   p.LastName
FROM HumanResources.Employee e
INNER JOIN Person.Person p
ON p.BusinessEntityID = e.BusinessEntityID
WHERE FirstName LIKE 'E%'
```

We can force a MERGE JOIN in the join predicate:

```
SELECT
   e.BusinessEntityID,
   p.Title,
   p.FirstName,
   p.LastName
FROM HumanResources.Employee e
INNER MERGE JOIN Person.Person p
ON p.BusinessEntityID = e.BusinessEntityID
WHERE FirstName LIKE 'E%'
```

We might get far better performance with some circumstances, but others may prove poor in performance terms. Considering the query is quite simple, the execution plan is not very pretty. The join type's index usage is limited, resulting in an index recommendation where one probably isn't needed.

When you force a MERGE JOIN, you add extra operators to the execution plan to ensure outputs needed to resolve the result set are properly sorted.

```
A HASH JOIN can also be forced:
SELECT
   e.BusinessEntityID,
   p.Title,
   p.FirstName,
   p.LastName
FROM HumanResources.Employee e
INNER HASH JOIN Person.Person p
ON p.BusinessEntityID = e.BusinessEntityID
WHERE FirstName LIKE 'E%'
```

Once again, we have an ugly plan. In the output tab, there is a warning telling us that our join choice has enforced the join order. This is quite important because it lets us know that our chosen join type has placed a limit on how many ways the tables can be ordered throughout the optimization. Essentially, what we did was take away many tools the query optimizer should have been able to use, forcing it to work with a limited selection, not enough to succeed.

If the hints are removed, the optimizer chooses a NESTED LOOP join, providing much better performance.

We often use hints as quick fixes to complicated problems, but they are typically used only as a last resort while there are some good reasons to use them. This is because they are extra elements in the query that need to be maintained and reviews as code, schema, and data changes.

If you do need to use them, you must document their use. After all, in three years, a developer is unlikely to know why you used a hint unless it has been documented.

In Chapter five, we'll look at how to use the rule-based optimizer.

Chapter 5

Using the Rule-Based Optimizer

While you should use the cost-based approach (discussed later), it's only fair to give you an overview of the rule-based optimizer. Oracle still supports the RBO, but new applications should be designed with the CBO, which should also be used to data warehouse applications because it supports enhanced DSS features.

Let's dive in.

In these three scenarios:

- OPTIMIZER_MODE=CHOOSE

- Where there are no statistics

- If hints are not added

The SQL statement will use RBO, which can be used to access object types and relational data.

In these three scenarios:

- OPTIMIZER_MODE=FIRST_ROWS

- FIRST_ROWS_n, or

- ALL_ROWS

- And no existing statistics

The CBO uses the default statistics.

The CBO can be enabled on a trial basis, just through the collection of statistics. Then, if you delete the statistics, you can go back to the RBO. You can also return to the RBO if you set the OPTIMIZER_MODE initialization parameter values or the ALTER SESSION statement's OPTIMIZER_MODE clause to RULE. This value can also be used to collect data statistics and examine them without using CBO.

Understanding the RBO Access Paths

With the rule-based approach, the execution plan chosen by the optimizer is based on the available access paths and their ranks. Oracle uses a heuristic approach to rank the access paths. If an SQL statement can be executed in more than one way, the RBO will always choose the lowest-ranked operation as these tend to execute faster than the higher-ranked ones.

Below you can see the paths with their ranking:

- **RBO Path 1** – Single Row by Rowid

- **RBO Path 2** - Single Row by Cluster Join

- **RBO Path 3** - Single Row by Hash Cluster Key with Unique or Primary Key

- **RBO Path 4** - Single Row by Unique or Primary Key

- **RBO Path 5** - Clustered Join

- **RBO Path 6** - Hash Cluster Key

- **RBO Path 7** - Indexed Cluster Key

- **RBO Path 8** - Composite Index

- **RBO Path 9** - Single-Column Indexes

- **RBO Path 10** - Bounded Range Search on Indexed Columns

- **RBO Path 11** - Unbounded Range Search on Indexed Columns

- **RBO Path 12** - Sort Merge Join

- **RBO Path 13** - MAX or MIN of Indexed Column

- **RBO Path 14** - ORDER BY on Indexed Column

- **RBO Path 15** - Full Table Scan

Let's look at these in a bit more detail by describing them, indicating when each path is available and what output we can expect from the EXPLAIN PLAN.

RBO Path 1: Single Row by Rowid

This path will only be available when a WHERE clause in a statement has used rowid to identify the relevant rows or by using the Oracle Precompiler-supported SQL syntax of CURRENT OF CURSOR. The statement is accessed when rowid is used to access the table:

For example:

```
SELECT * FROM emp WHERE ROWID =
'AAAA7bAA5AAAA1UAAA';
```

The EXPLAIN PLAN output for this statement might look like this:

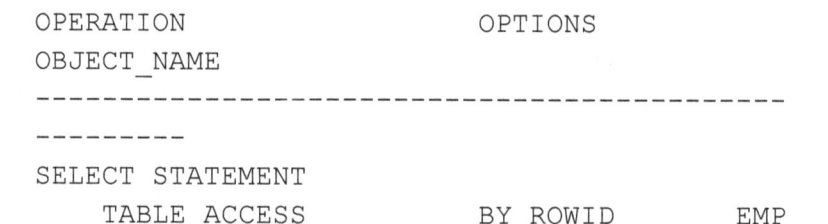

```
OPERATION                       OPTIONS
OBJECT_NAME
-------------------------------------------------
---------
SELECT STATEMENT
    TABLE ACCESS                BY ROWID         EMP
```

RBO Path 2: Single Row by Cluster Join

This path will be available for statements used to join those tables in the same cluster, provided the following conditions are true:

- The WHERE clause in the statement has conditions equating each cluster key column in a single table and the corresponding column in another.

- The WHERE clause also has a condition guaranteeing only one row will be returned by the join. This is most likely to be an equality condition on the primary or unique key's column/s.

AND operators must be used with these conditions, and Oracle will do a nested loops operation to execute the statement.

In the statement below, two tables, called dept and emp, are clustered on the column named deptno. The emp table's primary key is the empno column:

```
SELECT *
  FROM emp, dept
  WHERE emp.deptno = dept.deptno
    AND emp.empno = 7900;
```

The EXPLAIN PLAN output looks like this:

```
OPERATION                       OPTIONS
OBJECT_NAME
------------------------------------------------
---------
SELECT STATEMENT
    NESTED LOOPS
        TABLE ACCESS            BY ROWID         EMP
        INDEX                   UNIQUE SCAN
PK_EMP
        TABLE ACCESS            CLUSTER
DEPT
```

The index enforcing the primary key is called pk_emp.

RBO Path 3: Single Row by Hash Cluster Key with Unique or Primary Key

This one relies on both the following conditions being true to be available:

- The WHERE clause uses all the hash cluster key's columns in the equality conditions. In the case of composite cluster keys, AND operators must be used with the equality conditions.

- Only one row is guaranteed to be returned. This is because the hash cluster key's columns are also used to make up the primary or unique key.

The cluster's hash function is applied to the cluster key value in the statement to get the hash values, which is then used to carry out a hash scan across the table.

For example, in the statement below, both line_items and orders tables are stored inside a hash cluster. The column called orderno is the orders table's primary and the cluster key.

```
SELECT *
    FROM orders
    WHERE orderno = 65118968;
```

The output from the EXPLAIN PLAN might look something like this:

```
OPERATION                       OPTIONS
OBJECT_NAME
```

```
------------------------------------------------
---------
SELECT STATEMENT
    TABLE ACCESS              HASH
ORDERS
```

RBO Path 4: *Single Row by Unique or Primary Key*

This path is only available when the WHERE clause uses all of the unique or primary key's columns in the equality conditions. AND operators are required with the equality conditions for the composite keys. The statement is executed by a unique scan on the unique or primary key's index, and a single rowid is retrieved and used to access the table.

In the statement below, the emp table's primary key is the empno column:

```
SELECT *
    FROM emp
    WHERE empno = 7900;
```

The output might look something like this:

```
OPERATION                         OPTIONS
OBJECT_NAME
------------------------------------------------
---------
SELECT STATEMENT
    TABLE ACCESS              BY ROWID        EMP
        INDEX                 UNIQUE SCAN
PK_EMP
```

The index enforcing the primary key is called pk_emp.

RBO Path 5: Clustered Join

This path is only available to statements joining tables stored in one cluster, should the WHERE clause have conditions equating the cluster key's columns from one table with another table's corresponding columns. Again, AND operators are needed for composter keys.

A nested loop operation is carried out to execute the statement. For example, in the statement below, the dept and emp tables are both clustered on the column named deptno:

```
SELECT *
    FROM emp, dept
    WHERE emp.deptno = dept.deptno;
```

The output would be something like this:

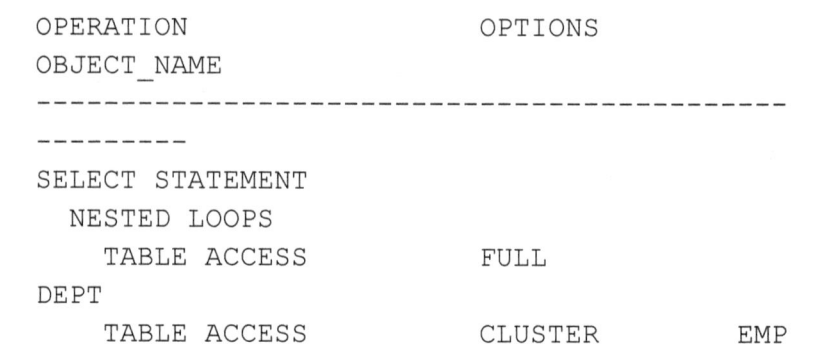

```
OPERATION                       OPTIONS
OBJECT_NAME
------------------------------------------------
---------
SELECT STATEMENT
  NESTED LOOPS
    TABLE ACCESS                FULL
DEPT
    TABLE ACCESS                CLUSTER         EMP
```

RBO Path 6: Hash Cluster Key

When a WHERE clause uses all the hash cluster key's columns in equality conditions, this access path will be available. As usual, the AND operators must be used for composite keys. Finally, the hash function from the cluster is applied to the cluster key value to get a hash value, which is then used to do a hash scan across the table.

In the next statement, the line_items and orders tables are stored in one hash cluster, while the cluster key is the orderno column:

```
SELECT *
    FROM line_items
    WHERE orderno = 65118968;
```

The output from the EXPLAIN PLAN would look like this:

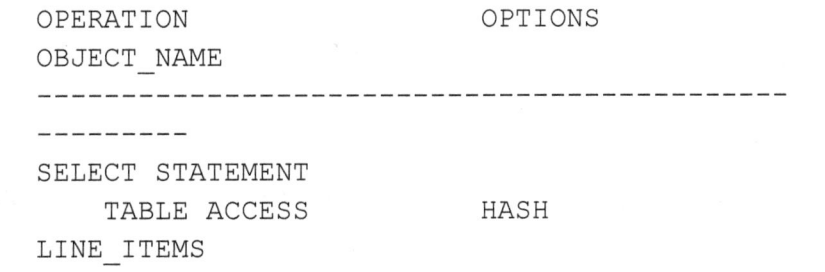

```
OPERATION                               OPTIONS
OBJECT_NAME
------------------------------------------------
---------
SELECT STATEMENT
    TABLE ACCESS                        HASH
LINE_ITEMS
```

RBO Path 7: Indexed Cluster Key

When the WHERE clause uses all the indexed cluster's key columns in equality conditions, the access path becomes available. The AND operator must be used with composite keys.

Executing the statement requires a unique scan to be done on the cluster index, retrieving a one-row rowid containing the specified cluster key value. That rowid is then used with a cluster scan to access the table. All the rows with identical cluster key values are together so that the scan can locate all of them with one rowid.

The statement below shows the emp table is stored in an indexed cluster with a cluster key of the deptno column:

```
SELECT *  FROM emp
   WHERE deptno = 10;
```

The output from the EXPLAIN PLAN would look like this:

```
OPERATION                          OPTIONS
OBJECT_NAME
-------------------------------------------
---------
SELECT STATEMENT
   TABLE ACCESS                    CLUSTER         EMP
      INDEX                        UNIQUE SCAN
PERS_INDEX
```

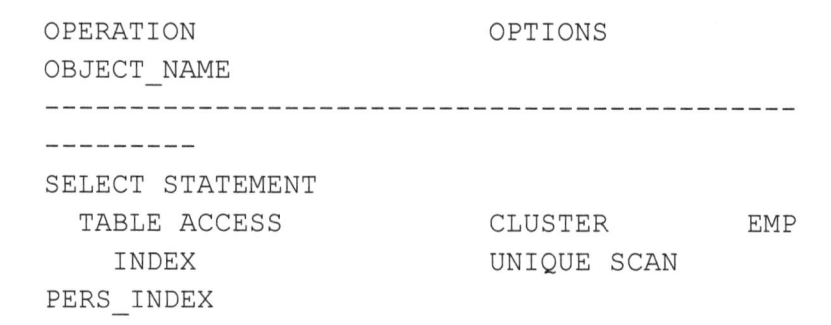

The cluster index is called pers_index

RBO Path 8: Composite Index

The path becomes available when the WHERE clause uses all the composite index's columns in the equality conditions, together with AND operators. First, the statement is executed by a range scan run on the index. Then, the rowids are retrieved for specified rows and used to access the table.

The statement below shows a composite index on two columns – deptno and job:

```
SELECT *
    FROM emp
    WHERE job = 'CLERK'
      AND deptno = 30;
```

The output from the EXPLAIN PLAN would look like this:

```
OPERATION                       OPTIONS
OBJECT_NAME
------------------------------------------------
---------
SELECT STATEMENT
    TABLE ACCESS                BY ROWID        EMP
        INDEX                   RANGE SCAN
JOB_DEPTNO_INDEX
```

The composite index on the deptno and job columns is called job_deptno_index.

RBO Path 9: Single-Column Indexes

This path becomes available when the WHERE clause uses all the columns of at least one single-column index in the equality conditions. AND operators must be used with the conditions for multiple indexes.

If the column from just one index is used, the statement is executed through a range scan, retrieving the specified rows' rowids from the index and using the rowids to access the table.

In the statement below, the emp table's job column has an index:

```
SELECT *
    FROM emp
    WHERE job = 'ANALYST';
```

The output from the EXPLAIN PLAN would look like this:

```
OPERATION                       OPTIONS
OBJECT_NAME
------------------------------------------------
---------
```

```
SELECT STATEMENT
    TABLE ACCESS              BY ROWID          EMP
        INDEX                 RANGE SCAN
JOB_INDEX
```

The emp.job index is called job_index.

If multiple single-column indexes are used, the statement is executed by each index being range scanned, retrieving the rowids from all the rows that satisfy the specific conditions.

Up to five indexes may be merged. When a WHERE clause uses all the columns in five or more single-column indexes, five are merged, and rowid is used to access the table. The resulting rows are then tested to determine if the remaining conditions are satisfied before they are returned.

In the next statement, both the deptno and job columns in the emp table have indexes:

```
SELECT *
    FROM emp
    WHERE job = 'ANALYST'
        AND deptno = 20;
```

The output from the EXPLAIN PLAN would look like this:

```
OPERATION                     OPTIONS
OBJECT_NAME
-----------------------------------------------------
---------
SELECT STATEMENT
    TABLE ACCESS              BY ROWID          EMP
        AND-EQUAL
```

```
            INDEX                    RANGE SCAN
    JOB_INDEX
              INDEX                  RANGE SCAN
    DEPTNO_INDEX
```

The operation called AND-EQUAL will merge all the rowids retrieved from the deptno_index and job_index scans. The result is one rowid set of rows satisfying the query.

RBO Path 10: Bounded Range Search on Indexed Columns

This path becomes available when the WHERE clause has a condition that uses a single-index column's column or at least one column from a composite index's leading portion:

```
column = expr

column >[=] expr AND column <[=] expr

column BETWEEN expr AND expr

column LIKE 'c%'
```

Each condition specified indexed values in a bounded range, and the statement can access the values. The range is bounded because the least and greatest values are satisfied by the conditions. A statement like this is executed by a range scan on the index and rowid used to access the table.

Should the expression, expr, reference an indexed column, the access path will not be available.

In the next statement, the emp table's sal column has an index:

```
    SELECT *
      FROM emp
      WHERE sal BETWEEN 2000 AND 3000;
```

The output from the EXPLAIN PLAN would look like this:

```
    OPERATION                    OPTIONS
    OBJECT_NAME
    ---------------------------------------------
    ---------
    SELECT STATEMENT
      TABLE ACCESS               BY ROWID           EMP
        INDEX                    RANGE SCAN
    SAL_INDEX
```

The index on emp.sal is called sal_index.

In the next statement, the ename column in the emp table has an index:

```
    SELECT *
      FROM emp
      WHERE ename LIKE 'S%';
```

RBO Path 11: Unbounded Range Search on Indexed Columns

When the WHERE clause has one of the conditions listed below, using a single-column index's column or at least one column from the composite index's leading portion:

```
    WHERE column >[=] expr

    WHERE column <[=] expr
```

Each condition specifies an unbounded index value range, and the statement can access these values. The range is unbounded because the least OR greatest values are specified – it cannot be both. A range scan is done on the index to execute the statements, and then rowid is used to access the table.

In the next statement, the emp table's sal column has an index:

```
SELECT *
    FROM emp
    WHERE sal > 2000;
```

The output from the EXPLAIN PLAN would look like this:

```
OPERATION                       OPTIONS
OBJECT_NAME
-------------------------------------------------
---------
SELECT STATEMENT
    TABLE ACCESS                BY ROWID        EMP
        INDEX                   RANGE SCAN
SAL_INDEX
```

The next statement shows a composite index on two columns in the line_items table – line and order:

```
SELECT *
    FROM line_items
    WHERE order > 65118968;
```

The WHERE clause makes use of the order column, which is a leading section of the index, ensuring the access path is available

In the next statement, the path isn't available. This statement has an index on the line and order columns.

87

```
SELECT *
    FROM line_items
    WHERE line < 4;
```

The reason it isn't available is that only the line column is used, and this isn't a leading section of the index.

RBO Path 12: Sort Merge Join

Access path 12 is available for those statements used for joining tables that aren't in a cluster together, should the WHERE clause use one or more columns from every joined table in the equality conditions. This statement is executed via a merge-sort operation, but Oracle may also execute a join statement using a nested loops operation.

The statement below shows the dept and emp tables not being stored in a cluster together:

```
SELECT *
    FROM emp, dept
    WHERE emp.deptno = dept.deptno;
```

The output from the EXPLAIN PLAN would look like this:

```
OPERATION                       OPTIONS
OBJECT_NAME
-------------------------------------------------
---------
SELECT STATEMENT
  MERGE JOIN
    SORT                        JOIN
      TABLE ACCESS              FULL            EMP
    SORT                        JOIN
```

```
TABLE ACCESS                FULL
DEPT
```

RBO Path 13: MAX or MIN of Indexed Column

This path is available for SELECT statements so long as ALL the conditions below are true:

- The maximum or minimum values of the single-column index column or a composite index's leading column are selected by the query using the MAX or MIN function. The index may not be a cluster, and the MAX or MIN function's argument should be an expression that involves one of the following:

    o The column

    o A constant

    o The addition operator - +

    o The CONCAT function

    o The concatenation operator - ||

- The SELECT list may not contain any other expressions

- There is no GROUP BY or WHERE clause in the statement

Oracle will do a full scan on the index the execute the query, retrieving the minimum or maximum indexed value. As this is the only value selected, Oracle doesn't need access to the table once the index is scanned.

In the next statement, the emp table's sal column has an index:

```
SELECT MAX(sal) FROM emp;
```

The output from the EXPLAIN PLAN would look like this:

```
     0         SELECT STATEMENT
Optimizer=CHOOSE
  1    0    SORT (AGGREGATE)
  2    1      INDEX (FULL SCAN (MIN/MAX)) OF
'SAL_INDEX' (NON-UNIQUE)
```

RBO Path 14: ORDER BY on Indexed Column

This path is available to SELECT statements so long as ALL the conditions below are true:

- An ORDER BY clause is in the query, using a single-column index's column OR a composite index's leading portion. The index may not be a cluster.

- A NOT NULL or PRIMARY KEY integrity constraint is in place, guaranteeing a minimum of one indexed column from the ORDER BY clause does not contain any nulls.

- The initialization parameter is BINARY for NLS_SORT.

The query is executed using an index range scan to ger the selected rows' rowids in a sorted order. The rowids are then used to access the table.

The statement below shows the emp table's empno column has a primary key:

```
SELECT *
    FROM emp
    ORDER BY empno;
```

The output from the EXPLAIN PLAN would look like this:

```
OPERATION                       OPTIONS
OBJECT_NAME
-------------------------------------------------
---------
SELECT STATEMENT
   TABLE ACCESS                 BY ROWID        EMP
      INDEX                     RANGE SCAN
PK_EMP
```

The index enforcing the primary key is called pk_emp. The primary key is used to ensure there are no nulls in the column.

RBO Path 15: Full Table Scan

This path is available to all SQL statements, no matter what conditions are in the WHERE clause. The only exception is when the FROM clause has SAMPLE BLOCK or SAMPLE in it.

The access path with the lowest ranking is the full table scan, meaning the RBO will always pick access paths that use indexes where one is available. This happens even when the full table scan would prove faster at execution.

Access paths are not available when the following conditions are in place:

- column1 > column2

- column1 < column2
- column1 >= column2
- column1 <= column2

Where column1 and column2 are found in one table.

- column IS NULL
- column IS NOT NULL
- column NOT IN
- column != expr
- column LIKE '%pattern'

Whether column has been indexed or not.

- expr = expr2

The expr expression operates on columns containing functions or operators, whether the column has been indexed or not.

- NOT EXISTS subquery
- ROWNUM pseudocolumn in a view
- Any condition with an un-indexed column

If an SQL statement only has these constructs and doesn't contain any that make the paths available, it must use a full table scan. The statement below accesses the emp table uses a full table scan:

```
SELECT *
    FROM emp;
```

The output from the EXPLAIN PLAN would look like this:

```
OPERATION               OPTIONS         OBJECT_NAME
---------------------------------------------------
SELECT STATEMENT
    TABLE ACCESS            FULL                EMP
```

Using RBO to Choose an Execution Plan for a Join

The considerations below apply to rule-based and cost-based approaches:

- First, the optimizer must determine whether a join between at least two tables will return a row source with a maximum of one row. Such situations are recognized by the optimizer based on PRIMARY KEY and UNIQUE table constraints. Should there be such a situation, these tables are put first in the join order before the rest of the table joins are optimized.

- Where a join statement contains outer join conditions, the table in the condition comes before the one with the outer join operator in the join order. Should any join order go against this rule, it will not be considered by the optimizer.

In the rule-based approach, the steps below are performed to pick the best execution plan for statements joining R tables:

With the rule-based approach, the optimizer performs the following steps to choose an execution plan for a statement that joins R tables:

- Each join order position must be filled, so the optimizer will choose a table with the highest-ranked access path per the ranking order discussed above. This step is repeated until all join positions are filled.

- The optimizer will also pick an operation that joins each table to the row source or previous table. The sort-merge operation is ranked as access path 11, and the following rules are applied:

  o If the chosen access path is 11 or better, a nested loops operation is chosen as the outer table, using the row source or previous table in the order.

  o If the access path is below 12 and an equijoin condition is in place between the chosen and previous row source or table, a sort-merge operation is chosen

  o If the access path is below 12 and there is no equijoin condition, a nested loops operation is chosen with the previous row source or table as the outer table.

- Next, the optimizer will choose a plan from the resulting set. The goal is to choose the right plan that maximizes how many nested loop join operations are used where an index scan is used to access the inner table. Nested loop joins access tables multiple times, so inner table scans improve their performance significantly.

- The optimizer will not typically consider the table order in the FROM clause when it picks an execution plan. Instead, the rules below are applied to choose the plan:

    o The execution plan with the least nested loop operations accessing the inner table with a full table scan;

    o Where two or more plans are tied, the optimizer picks the plan with the least number of sort-merge operations;

    o If there are still tied plans, the optimizer picks the one where the first table listed in the join order has the highest-ranked access path;

    o Where a tie exists between several plans where the access path for the single-column index access the first table in the order, the plan accessing the first table with the highest number of merged indexes is chosen;

- Where a tie exists between several plans where bounded range scans access the first tables, the plan where the highest number of composite index leading columns access the first table is chosen;

- If there still remains a tie, the execution plan chosen is the one where the FROM clause has the first table later in the query.

Using the RBO to Transform and Optimize Statements

SQL is one of the most flexible query languages, and there are lots of statements that achieve the same thing. On occasion, the optimizer will transform a statement into another that does the same thing, where the second statement offers more efficient execution.

Using RBO to Transform an OR into a Compound Query

If a WHERE clause in a query has several conditions with OR operators, the query is transformed into a compound query with a UNION ALL set operator, provided that query is more efficient to execute:

- If index access paths are made available by each condition, the transformation can happen. Then, an execution plan that can access the table several times with different indexes before producing a result set is chosen.

- If a full table scan is required by a condition because an index is not made available, the statement cannot be transformed. Instead, a full table scan executes the statement, and each table row is tested to see if any conditions are satisfied.

With the rule-based approach, the UNION ALL transformation is made by the optimizer. This is because an index can be used to execute the compound query's component query. Therefore, RBO will assume that it is faster to use two index scans to execute the query than using a full table scan.

Alternative SQL Syntax

While two different SQL statements can give us the same result, one may be processed faster than the other. The EXPLAIN PLAN results can be used to compare plans and the costs of the statements to see which one is the most efficient.

The next example details execution plans for two statements that do the same thing. They both return the dept table departments with no employees listed in the emp table. The emp table is searched by each statement using a subquery. For this example, assume that the emp table's deptno column contains an index called deptno_index.

Here is the first statement with its plan:

```
SELECT dname, deptno
   FROM dept
   WHERE deptno NOT IN
      (SELECT deptno FROM emp);
```

The transformed statement's execution plan may look like the illustration below. The shaded boxes indicate where data is physically retrieved, while the clear box indicates where operations are done on data that comes back from the previous step:

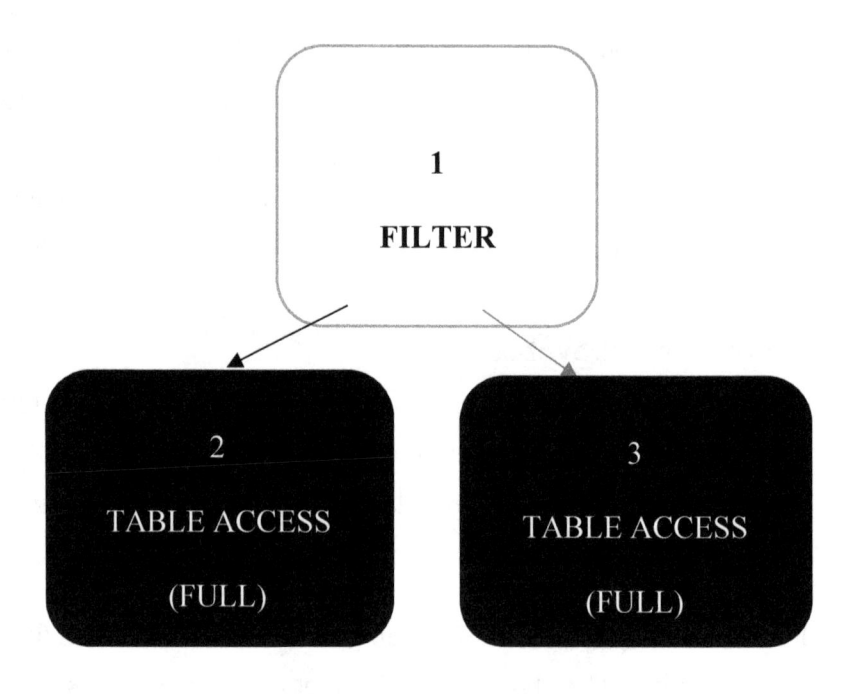

```
            1
         FILTER
       /        \
      2          3
  TABLE ACCESS  TABLE ACCESS
    (FULL)        (FULL)
```

In step three, the statement is executed through a full table scan of emp, regardless of the index present in deptno. This is time-consuming. The index is not used because the subquery searching the emp table has no WHERE clause to make the index available.

However, the statement below will access the index and choose the same rows:

```
SELECT dname, deptno
FROM dept
WHERE NOT EXISTS
     (SELECT deptno
     FROM emp
     WHERE dept.deptno = emp.deptno);
```

The transformed statement's execution plan may look something like the illustration below, with the shaded boxes for where data is physically retrieved and clear for operations on the data that comes back from the previous step:

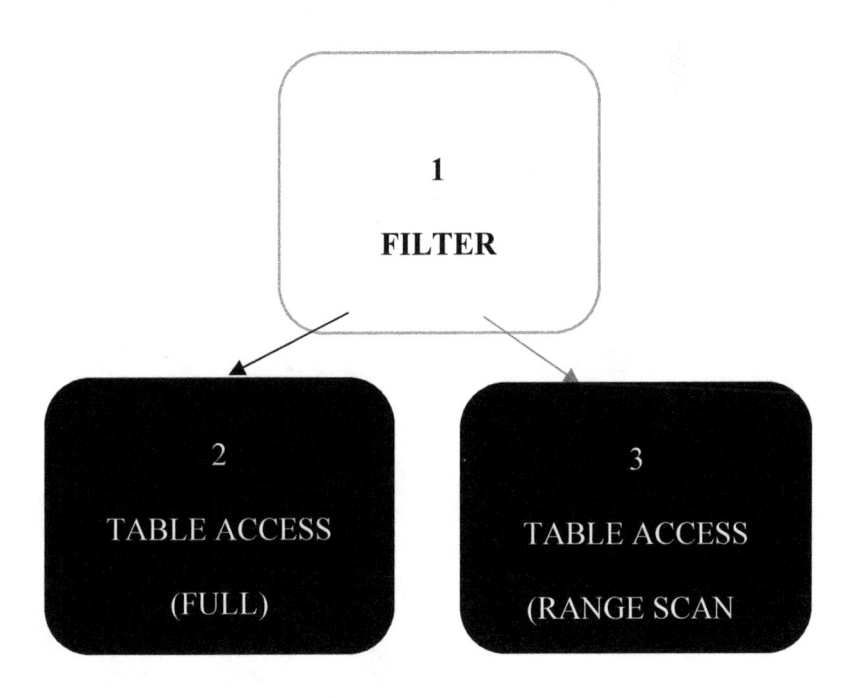

```
              1
           FILTER

   2                    3
TABLE ACCESS       TABLE ACCESS
  (FULL)           (RANGE SCAN
```

The subquery's WHERE clause references the emp table's deptno column, which is why deptno_index is used. This is reflected in the execution plan's third step. As a result, the index range scan takes less time than the first statement's full table scan, and the first query will fully scan the emp table for each deptno the dept table contains. This is why the second statement is faster.

Where application statements have a NOT IN operator, as seen in the statement above, you should rewrite them to use a NOT EXISTS operator, allowing the statements to use an existing index.

As a final note, be aware that alternative syntax is only effective when used with the rule-based optimizer.

In the next chapter, we will talk about using the Cost-Based optimizer and database statistics.

Chapter 6

Using the Cost-Based Optimizer and Database Statistics

When the SQL Server receives a valid statement for the first time, an execution plan is produced, describing the best way to retrieve the required data. In the early days, two optimizers were available to produce these plans:

- **Rule-Based Optimizer (RBO)** – the original method, RBO listed the rules to be followed in generating a plan. After CBO was released, RBO continued to be used where there were no internal statistics in the Server related to the objects the statement referenced or if a hint or session/instance parameter requested it. However, RBO has now been deprecated in newer versions.

- **Cost-Based Optimizer (CBO)** – the newest method, CBO generates execution plans by using database statistics. It chooses the lowest-cost plan, where the cost is related to the number of system resources the operation requires to complete. This is what we are discussing in this chapter.

In later versions of SQL Database, the only option is CBO. When a new object is created, the amount or spread of data in the database changes, meaning the real database state is not represented by the statistics. As such, the decision process the CBO goes through may be flawed. We're going to talk about managing statistics with the DBMS_STATS package.

If you were to put a dozen Oracle experts in a room together, most likely, they would all agree on one thing. They will say that database statistics are a critical factor in the cost-based optimizer's choice of execution plan. What they won't agree on is how those statistics are gathered.

A couple of quotes are particularly meaningful:

> *"You don't necessarily need up-to-date statistics. You need statistics that are representative of your data."*
> *- Graham Wood.*

This means that it isn't so important how old your statistics are. It's more important that they still represent the data. Looking at the DBA_TABLES view, at the column called LAST_ANALYZED, does not give you an indication of valid statistics.

> *"Do you want the optimizer to give you the best performance, or consistent performance?" - Anjo Kolk*

This means that changing your stats regularly can bring change, and that isn't always good.

Not for one minute do these experts suggest that your stats are never updated. They are merely pointing that when you do, you change the information the optimizer needs to use to decide on an execution plan. When you change the information, the optimizer will most likely choose a different plan and, while it will still hopefully be the right one, there is always a chance it won't. By gathering statistics for all your tables daily, your system may act differently each day, and this is one of the primary paradoxes of statistics gathering.

So, what kind of strategy should you have for statistics? Try these:

- **Automatic Optimizer Statistics Collection**

Later versions of the Oracle Database will gather the statistics automatically every day. Over the years, the default statistics job has come under fire, but its value is almost entirely dependent on the systems being managed. Much criticism has come from those talking about large data warehouses and other edge cases. If you have multiple small databases that don't require huge amounts of performance, Oracle can be left alone to do its job with the statistics. Specific problems can then be dealt with as they arise.

- **A Mixed Approach**

Most of your statistics collection is done by the automatic job, but some things have specific requirements, such as some schemas or tables. For those, you have a choice – set the object's preferences or lock down the stats so the automatic job can't change them. Then you can come up with a customized solution.

- **Manual**

Automatic stats collection is disabled, and you develop a customized solution for the entire database.

Which of these you do is dependent on each case but, no matter which one it is, your stats will be managed by the DBMS_STATS package. No matter which approach you choose, there are some things the automatic job will not gather, and these must be taken care of by you. Those are the fixed and system objects for all databases.

DBMS_STATS

DBMS_STATS came into play in Oracle 8i and is now the preferred Oracle method for statistics gathering. According to Oracle, there are several benefits to using this package, including long-term statistics storage, parallel execution, and transferring statistics between servers.

DBMS_STATS has differing functionality, depending on the database version you use, and so do the default parameter settings and statistics quality. For more detailed information, you should check out the document for your database version.

Table and Index Stats

We can gather table statistics for the schema, database, table, or partition:

```
EXEC DBMS_STATS.gather_database_stats;
```

```
EXEC
DBMS_STATS.gather_database_stats(estimate_pe
rcent => 15);
EXEC
DBMS_STATS.gather_database_stats(estimate_pe
rcent => 15, cascade => TRUE);

EXEC
DBMS_STATS.gather_schema_stats('SCOTT');
EXEC DBMS_STATS.gather_schema_stats('SCOTT',
estimate_percent => 15);
EXEC DBMS_STATS.gather_schema_stats('SCOTT',
estimate_percent => 15, cascade => TRUE);

EXEC DBMS_STATS.gather_table_stats('SCOTT',
'EMPLOYEES');
EXEC DBMS_STATS.gather_table_stats('SCOTT',
'EMPLOYEES', estimate_percent => 15);
EXEC DBMS_STATS.gather_table_stats('SCOTT',
'EMPLOYEES', estimate_percent => 15, cascade
=> TRUE);

EXEC DBMS_STATS.gather_dictionary_stats;
```

ESTIMATE_PERCENT is an often-used parameter for gathering statistics from bigger segments to decrease sample size, reducing the operation's overheads. From Oracle 9I onwards, we were also given the choice of allowing Oracle to use a constant called AUTO_SAMPLE_SIZE to determine sample size. However, this got something of a bad rap because Oracle didn't always choose an appropriate sample size, bringing the results into question.

From Oracle 11g, however, the AUTO_SAMPLE_SIZE constant became the default and preferred sample size because the mechanism that determined the actual size was improved. Not only that, but the statistics estimates are as near to 100% accurate as they can be and faster to gather too.

The parameter used to determine whether we should gather statistics for all the indexes on the currently analyzed table is the CASCADE parameter. In earlier database versions, the default was set to FALSE but, from 10g onwards, it is AUTO_CASCADE. This means that Oracle will decide whether the index statistics are required or not.

These modifications to how stats gathering behaves have led to the basic defaults for table stats being satisfactory in most cases.

We can use a procedure called GATHER_INDEX_STATS to gather index statistics explicitly:

```
EXEC DBMS_STATS.gather_index_stats('SCOTT',
'EMPLOYEES_PK');
EXEC DBMS_STATS.gather_index_stats('SCOTT',
'EMPLOYEES_PK', estimate_percent => 15);
```

Current information about statistics is found in the specific objects' dictionary data views – ALL, DBA, and USER. The following views were brought in with later Oracle releases:

- DBA_TABLES

- DBA_TAB_STATISTICS

- DBA_TAB_PARTITIONS

- DBA_TAB_SUB_PARTITIONS
- DBA_TAB_COLUMNS
- DBA_TAB_COL_STATISTICS
- DBA_PART_COL_STATISTICS
- DBA_SUBPART_COL_STATISTICS
- DBA_INDEXES
- DBA_IND_STATISTICS
- DBA_IND_PARTITIONS
- DBA_IND_SUBPARTIONS

And you can get histogram details from these views:

- DBA_TAB_HISTOGRAMS
- DBA_PART_HISTOGRAMS
- DBA_SUBPART_HISTOGRAMS

If you need to delete statistics for indexes, columns, or tables, use the following procedures:

```
EXEC DBMS_STATS.delete_database_stats;
EXEC DBMS_STATS.delete_schema_stats('SCOTT');
EXEC DBMS_STATS.delete_table_stats('SCOTT', 'EMP');
```

```
EXEC DBMS_STATS.delete_column_stats('SCOTT',
'EMP', 'EMPNO');
EXEC DBMS_STATS.delete_index_stats('SCOTT',
'EMP_PK');

EXEC DBMS_STATS.delete_dictionary_stats;
```

System Stats

From Oracle 9iRi, a different procedure was used to gather the statistics related to the system I/O and CPU performance – GATHER_SYSTEM_STATS. Providing the optimizer with this kind of information allows it to be more accurate in its choice of an execution plan because it can weigh up the costs of using the I/O and CPU system profiles.

There are two types of possible system statistics:

Noworkload – Every database has a default set of these statistics, but we can replace them with better, more accurate details. When noworkload stats are gathered, a random series of I/Os is issued, and the database tests the CPU speed. As you would expect, this loads your system while it is gathering statistics:

```
EXEC DBMS_STATS.gather_system_stats;
```

Workload – When the interval or start/stop parameters are used to initiate this, counters are used to track the system operations, providing an accurate picture of system performance. Where available, workload statistics are used over noworkload statistics.

-- Manually start and stop to sample a representative time (several hours) of system activity.

```
EXEC
DBMS_STATS.gather_system_stats('start');
EXEC DBMS_STATS.gather_system_stats('stop');
```

-- Sample from now until a specific number of minutes.

```
DBMS_STATS.gather_system_stats('interval',
interval => 180);
```

You can use the table called AUX_STATS$ to show your current system stats:

```
SELECT pname, pval1 FROM sys.aux_stats$
WHERE sname = 'SYSSTATS_MAIN';

PNAME                              PVAL1
------------------------------ ----------
CPUSPEED
CPUSPEEDNW                          1074
IOSEEKTIM                             10
IOTFRSPEED                          4096
MAXTHR
MBRC
MREADTIM
SLAVETHR
SREADTIM

9 rows selected.

SQL>
```

The procedure called DELETE_SYSTEM_STATS is used to delete workload statistics and put default values in place of previous noworkload statistics.

```
EXEC DBMS_STATS.delete_system_stats;
```

Your system statistics only need updating when your workload profile or system hardware has been majorly changed.

System statistics tend to draw two schools of thought. The first is to avoid using them entirely, sticking to the default noworkload statistics. The second is to ensure accurate statistics are provided. However, this comes with a problem because it isn't easy to determine a representation of accurate stats. As a result, many prefer to use a combination of methods to investigate their systems, including gathering all the stats into one table and using SET_SYSTEM_STATS to set the statistics manually:

```
EXEC
DBMS_STATS.set_system_stats('iotfrspeed',
4096);
```

If you are in any doubt about what to use, stick with the defaults.

Fixed Object Stats

In Oracle 10gR1, a procedure called GATHER_FIXED_OBJECTS_STATS was introduced to gather the stats on X$ tables. These are found beneath the V$ dynamic performance views. Truthfully, X$ are not really tables. They are more of a window to the Oracle kernel's memory structures. Fixed object stats must be gathered manually as they are not included in the automatic gathering, and this must be done when the database is at a representative activity level:

```
EXEC DBMS_STATS.gather_fixed_objects_stats;
```

When there are significant changes to system activity or initialization parameters, it is a signal that fresh stats should be gathered. However, under normal running, you don't have to do this regularly.

The DELETE_FIXED_OBJECTS_STATS procedure is used to remove the stats:

```
EXEC DBMS_STATS.delete_fixed_objects_stats;
```

Locking Stats

There are three levels at which stats can be locked to stop them from being overwritten – partition, schema, or table:

```
EXEC DBMS_STATS.lock_schema_stats('SCOTT');
EXEC DBMS_STATS.lock_table_stats('SCOTT',
'EMP');
EXEC
DBMS_STATS.lock_partition_stats('SCOTT',
'EMP', 'EMP_PART1');
```

Stats need to be unlocked before you can replace them:

```
EXEC
DBMS_STATS.unlock_schema_stats('SCOTT');
EXEC DBMS_STATS.unlock_table_stats('SCOTT',
'EMP');
EXEC
DBMS_STATS.unlock_partition_stats('SCOTT',
'EMP', 'EMP_PART1');
```

Locking stats is useful when you want to stop them from being changed by automated jobs, particularly with tables that ETL processes use. However, if the tables are empty when the stats are gathered, they will not accurately reflect the real data quality used for the load process. So instead, stats should be gathered on a full table once and then locked or every time data gets loaded.

Transferring Stats

Statistics can be transferred between servers to allow for consistent execution plans with different data amounts, but the statistics must first be gathered into a table. In the examples below, the APPSCHEMA user stats are pulled into a table called STATS_TABLE, which DBASCHEMA owns:

```
EXEC
DBMS_STATS.create_stat_table('DBASCHEMA','STATS_TABLE');
EXEC
DBMS_STATS.export_schema_stats('APPSCHEMA','STATS_TABLE',NULL,'DBASCHEMA');
```

You can then transfer the table to a different server using whatever method you prefer – SQL*PLUS COPY, Export/Import, etc. The stats will be imported as follows into the data dictionary:

```
EXEC
DBMS_STATS.import_schema_stats('APPSCHEMA','STATS_TABLE',NULL,'DBASCHEMA');
EXEC
DBMS_STATS.drop_stat_table('DBASCHEMA','STATS_TABLE');
```

Setting Preferences

From Oracle 10g onwards, many DBMS_STATS parameters' default values changed to using preferences from being hard-coded.

WE can use the SET_PARAM procedure to change these preferences:

EXEC DBMS_STATS.set_param('DEGREE', '5');

SET_PARAM was deprecated in 11g, replaced with a layered preferences approach. There are four preferences levels, amended using these procedures:

- **SET_GLOBAL_PREFS** - sets global preferences, which includes specific ones for automatic stats collection.

- **SET_DATABASE_PREFS** - sets the entire database's preferences.

- **SET_SCHEMA_PREFS** - sets a specific schema's preferences.

- **SET_TABLE_PREFS** – sets a specific table's preferences.

The table below shows the preferences with their available scope:

- G – Global

- D – Database

- S – Schema

- T – Table

Preference	Description	Default	Scope
AUTOSTATS_TARGET	Decides the objects that stats have been gathered for – AUTO, ORACLE, ALL	AUTO	G
CASCADE	Decides whether the current table's index stats should be gathered – TRUE, FALSE, AUTO_CASCADE	DBMS_STATS.AUTO_CASCADE	G, D, S, T
CONCURRENT	Decides whether stats should be gathered on multiple objects simultaneously or individually – AUTOMATIC, MANUAL, OFF, ALL	OFF	G
DEGREE	The degree of parallelism – DEFAULT_DEGREE or integer	DBMS_STATS.DEFAULT_DEGREE	G, D, S, T
ESTIMATE_PERCENT	Rows to sample percentage when stats-gathering – AUTO_SAMPLE_SIZE or 0.000001-100	DBMS_STATS.AUTO_SAMPLE_SIZE	G, D, S, T
GLOBAL_TEMP_TABLE_STATS	Decides whether global temporary table stats should be specific to a session or shared between sessions – SHARED, SESSION	SESSION	G, D, S
GRANULARITY			

114

GRANULARITY	Determines of partitioned object stats – ALL, DEFAULT, AUTO, GLOBAL, PARTITION, 'GLOBAL AND PARTITION,' SUBPARTITION	AUTO	G, D, S, T
INCREMENTAL	Decides is incremental stats should be used on partitioned objects for global stats or whether table scans should generate them – TRUE, FALSE	FALSE	G, D, S, T
INCREMENTAL_LEVEL	Determine the synopses level for collection on incremental partitioned stats – PARTITION, TABLE	PARTITION	G, D, S, T
INCREMENTAL_STALENESS	Determines how partition statistics staleness is determined – USE_LOCKED_STATE, USE_STALE_PERCENT,NULL	NULL	G, D, S, T
METHOD_OPT	Controls histogram creation and collection of column statistics	FOR ALL COLUMNS SIZE AUTO	G,D, S, T
NO_INVALIDATE	Decides whether to invalidate dependent cursors when there are new stats on objects – AUTO_INVALIDATE, TRUE, FALSE	DBMS_STATS.AUTO_INVALIDATE	G, D, S, T

OPTIONS	Used for the GATHER_TABLE_STATS procedure's OPTIONS parameter – GATHER AUTO, GATHER	GATHER	G,D, S, T
PUBLISH	Decides whether to publish gathered states straight away or leave them pending – TRUE, FALSE	TRUE	G, D, S, T
TABLE_CACHED_BLOCKS	Indicates how many blocks are cached in the buffer cache while the index cluster factor is being calculated – the recommended number is 16	1	G,D, S, T

Below you can see their basic use:

```
EXEC
DBMS_STATS.set_global_prefs('AUTOSTATS_TARGET', 'AUTO');
EXEC
DBMS_STATS.set_database_prefs('STALE_PERCENT', '15');
EXEC
DBMS_STATS.set_schema_prefs('SCOTT','DEGREE', '5');
EXEC DBMS_STATS.set_table_prefs('SCOTT', 'EMP', 'CASCADE', 'FALSE');
```

You can reset global preferences and delete other preference layers with these procedures:

```
EXEC DBMS_STATS.reset_global_pref_defaults;
EXEC
DBMS_STATS.delete_database_prefs('CASCADE');
EXEC
DBMS_STATS.delete_schema_prefs('SCOTT','DEGR
EE');
EXEC DBMS_STATS.delete_table_prefs('SCOTT',
'EMP', 'CASCADE');
```

Manually Setting Stats

There are several procedures in the DBMS_STATS package to help you set statistics manually:

- SET_SYSTEM_STATS
- SET_TABLE_STATS
- SET_COLUMN_STATS
- SET_INDEX_STATS

You can return current stats with these procedures:

- GET_SYSTEM_STATS
- GET_TABLE_STATS
- GET_COLUMN_STATS
- GET_INDEX_STATS

When you set stats manually, you must be careful. One of the best and potentially safest ways is to retrieve the current values first.

Then they can be amended as needed and set. Below, you can see an example showing you how to set column stats:

```
SET SERVEROUTPUT ON
DECLARE
  l_distcnt   NUMBER;
  l_density   NUMBER;
  l_nullcnt   NUMBER;
  l_srec      DBMS_STATS.StatRec;
  l_avgclen   NUMBER;
BEGIN
  -- Get current values.
  DBMS_STATS.get_column_stats (
    ownname => 'SCOTT',
    tabname => 'EMP',
    colname => 'EMPNO',
    distcnt => l_distcnt,
    density => l_density,
    nullcnt => l_nullcnt,
    srec    => l_srec,
    avgclen => l_avgclen);

  -- Amend values.
  l_srec.minval  - =
UTL_RAW.cast_from_number(7369);
  l_srec.maxval  - =
UTL_RAW.cast_from_number(7934);

  -- Set new values.
  DBMS_STATS.set_column_stats (
    ownname => 'SCOTT',
    tabname => 'EMP',
    colname => 'EMPNO',
    distcnt => l_distcnt,
    density => l_density,
    nullcnt => l_nullcnt,
```

```
            srec     => l_srec,
            avgclen => l_avgclen);
END;
/
```

The issues you may need to deal with include:

- Dataload tables may need to be excluded from regular stats unless you definitely know they will be full when it's time to gather the stats

- Before Oracle 10g, you may find stats gathering for the SYS schema slows your system down

- Statistics gathering is heavy on resources for the server, so try to gather only stale stats or collect at off-peak workload times

- Even if your gathering procedure is scheduled, you may need to do it again after large data loads of database maintenance.

Scheduling Stats

Before Oracle 10g, you could ensure your statistics were up to date by using the DBMS_JOB package to schedule the statistics gathering.

```
SET SERVEROUTPUT ON
DECLARE
  l_job   NUMBER;
BEGIN
  DBMS_JOB.submit(l_job,
```

```
                    'BEGIN
DBMS_STATS.gather_schema_stats(''SCOTT'');
END;',
                    SYSDATE,
                    'SYSDATE + 1');
   COMMIT;
   DBMS_OUTPUT.put_line('Job - ' || l_job);
END;
/
```

This code sets the job up to gather statics for the current daily time for SCOTT. The current jobs can be listed on the server using two views – DBA_JOBS and DBA_JOBS RUNNING.

If you want to remove existing jobs, use the statant below, where X indicates the job to be removed.

```
EXEC DBMS_JOB.remove(X);
COMMIT;
```

In the next chapter, we'll look at execution plans in more detail and learn how we can use them to speed things up.

Chapter 7

Reading an Execution Plan

You've got your SQL query ready to go, and you are happy to sit back and let it do its thing. But you keep sitting and waiting as your query grinds its slow and torturous way to the end.

How do you make your queries faster?

SQL greatest power lies in its declarative nature. You tell it what you want, and it will work out how to get it. But that's just the database deciding HOW the query should be executed. It doesn't tell you how to speed it up.

The answer to this question lies in how your tables are accessed and joined – this information can let you see if a better approach exists but, to get that information, you need the execution plan.

We discussed execution plans previously, but now we'll go into more detail and talk about reading one and using it to speed up your SQL.

What Is An Execution Plan?

First, a quick discussion on plans. There are two database plans – execution and explain. The EXPLAIN plan predicts what could happen when your query runs. It could be a wrong prediction for so many reasons, and improving code performance requires knowing what really went on with the query.

The execution plan provides the steps taken by the database when it ran the query, including information such as:

- Key metrics, which help with tuning

- The number of rows returned

- What I/O was used for processing

- Execution time

And much more.

So, what is this execution plan, and how does it work?

When a query goes to the database, the SQL optimizer must determine how to execute it. To do that, SQL creates the execution plan. Think of it as being GPS directions to get you to your destination. Instead of telling you when to turn and which route you need to take, it tells you how your tables should be accessed and the order to do it in. For example, it will tell you to join tables 1 and 2 and then join them to table 3.

By seeing which route the database went, you can see if it was the best path or if you need to add a shortcut to make it go a different, more efficient use.

Below, you can see an execution plan that joins two tables:

```
----------------------------------------
| Id  | Operation            | Name    |
----------------------------------------
|  0  | SELECT STATEMENT     |         |
|  1  |  HASH JOIN           |         |
|  2  |   TABLE ACCESS FULL| COLORS   |
|  3  |   TABLE ACCESS FULL| BRICKS   |
----------------------------------------
```

Every line in an execution plan is an individual operation, and they are all linked using a parent-child relationship, common in computer programing.

An execution plan is an upside-down tree. At the top, you have the root, the SELECT statement. At the bottom, you have the leaves, your tables, and between are all the possible operations. Those operations come under three categories:

- Single-child operations

- Multi-child operations

- Joins

The single-child operation will only have one operation beneath it in the plan, such as sorting and grouping steps. The multi-child operation is not common, but it will have one or more operations when used, such as UNION (ALL). Lastly, JOINs will always have two children, no more, no less. They may be tables, joins, or some other operation.

Reading an Execution Plan

When you read a text-based plan, you will notice that parts of the code are indented. This indicates the parent-child relationship. The parent is on the first line, eft-indented, while the child/children are below, right-indented.

The two-join plan in the earlier example could also be drawn to look like this:

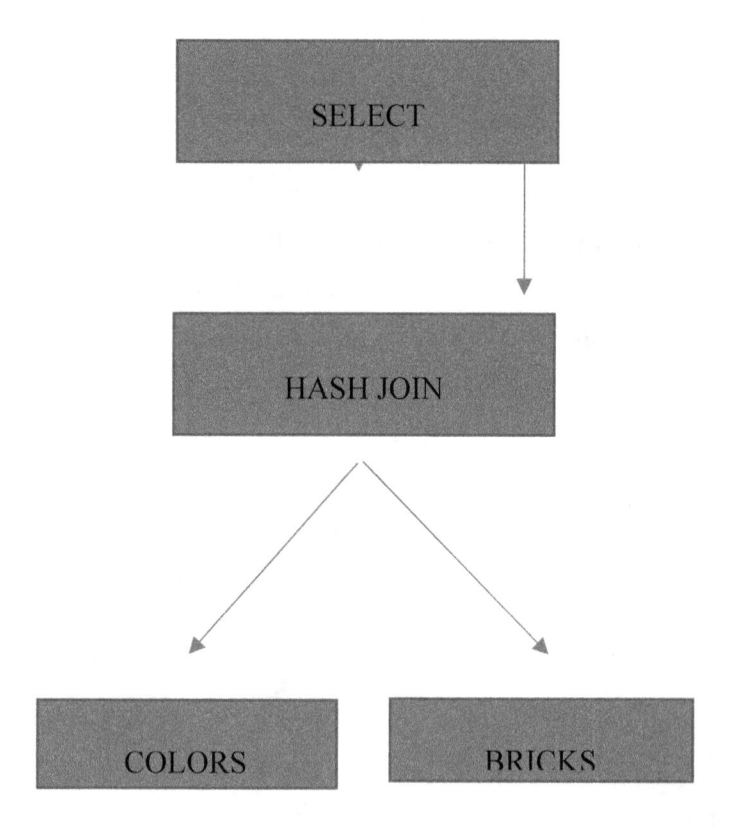

```
        SELECT
           |
           v
       HASH JOIN
        /      \
       v        v
    COLORS    BRICKS
```

The database does a depth-first search to follow a plan. This search starts at the top and traverses the tree to the first leaf. Then, it goes back up the tree, stopping at the first operation that has an unvisited child.

The process is repeated, back down to the second leaf and back up to the next operation with the unvisited child. This goes on until all the steps in the plan have been read.

In this case, the two-table join execution plan has the following order of operations:

1. Starting at the top with the SELECT statement, it traverses to the first leaf. This is the COLORS table's TABLE ACCESS FULL.

2. The rows from this table are passed to the HASH JOIN, the first leaf's parent.

3. The next unvisited child of the first step is found, the BRICKS table's TABLE ACCESS FULL

4. This table's rows are passed to the parent, which is HASH JOIN

5. All of the first step's children are accessed, so the surviving rows from the JOIN to the SELECT statement operation are passed to the client.

NOTE

Data always flow UP, from the plan's leaves to its roots.

Have a look at another example, this time a four-table join:

```
------------------------------------------
| Id | Operation            | Name       |
------------------------------------------
|  0 | SELECT STATEMENT     |            |
|  1 |  HASH JOIN           |            |
|  2 |   HASH JOIN          |            |
|  3 |    HASH JOIN         |            |
|  4 |     TABLE ACCESS FULL| COLORS     |
|  5 |     TABLE ACCESS FULL| TOYS       |
|  6 |    TABLE ACCESS FULL | PENS       |
|  7 |   TABLE ACCESS FULL  | BRICKS     |
------------------------------------------
```

The order of operations in this is:

1. Starting from the top at the SELECT statement, we traverse to the first leaf. Again, the is the COLORS table's TABLE FULL ACCESS, as you can see in step four of the plan.

2. The rows from this table are passed to the HASH JOIN in step three, which is the first parent's leaf.

3. The next unvisited child is located, the TOYS table's TABLE ACCESS FULL, in step five.

4. The rows are passed to HASH JOIN in step three. Because step three doesn't have any other children, we go back to the

126

rows that survive step three's HASH JOIN and pass them to step two's HASH JOIN.

5. Search for step two's next child, which is the PENS table's TABLE ACCESS FULL, in step six.

6. These rows are passed to step two's HASH JOIN, and because there are no more children for step two, the surviving rows go to the HASH JOIN in step one.

7. This is repeated until all operations are run.

So, access the step IDs in the execution plan is in this order – 4, 3, 5, 3, 2, 6, 2, 1, 7, 1, 0.

Advanced Examples

Up to now, we have used straightforward joins in our examples so let's now look at a more complicated example containing single-child and multi-child operations:

```
-------------------------------------------
| Id | Operation               | Name    |
-------------------------------------------
|  0 | SELECT STATEMENT        |         |
|  1 |  SORT ORDER BY          |         |
|  2 |   HASH GROUP BY         |         |
|  3 |    HASH JOIN            |         |
|  4 |     TABLE ACCESS FULL   | COLORS  |
|  5 |     VIEW                |         |
|  6 |      UNION-ALL          |         |
|  7 |       TABLE ACCESS FULL | BRICKS  |
|  8 |       TABLE ACCESS FULL | TOYS    |
|  9 |       TABLE ACCESS FULL | PENS    |
```

You might think this is way more complicated, but it follows the same process to read it.

1. Traverse down to the first leaf, which is the COLORS table's TABLE ACCESS FULL in step four.

2. Pass this table's rows up the plan to the first leaf's parents, which is the HASH JOIN in step three.

3. Locate the next leaf, the BRICKS table's TABLE ACCESS FULL, in step seven.

4. This has a parent of UNION ALL, which is a multi-child operation. That means the database will go on to execute steps eight and nine. *

5. The rows from the tables in steps seven, eight, and nine are passed to UNION ALL in step six, combining all the rows into a single dataset.

6. Traverse up the tree to HASH JOIN in step three

7. The rows from steps four and six are joined, and the surviving rows passed to HASH GROUP BY in step two.

8. The grouped rows are returned to SORT ORDER BY in step one.

9. Lastly, the data is returned to the client.

* An optimization called concurrent execution of UNION ALL helps the database run the table scans simultaneously in parallel queries.

The Exception Proving the Rule

We've looked at operations and key plan types in the previous examples but, when it comes to the optimizer and the execution plans, there are also edge cases. Our last example breaks the rule from the other examples where the first leaf is first.

```
-----------------------------------------
| Id | Operation          | Name    |
-----------------------------------------
|  0 | SELECT STATEMENT   |         |
|  1 |  SORT AGGREGATE    |         |
|  2 |   TABLE ACCESS FULL| BRICKS  |
|  3 |   TABLE ACCESS FULL| COLORS  |
-----------------------------------------
```

You should be able to spot at a glance what's wrong – there isn't a JOIN operation. Why not?

In the SELECT statement for this query's plan, there is a scalar subquery:

```
select (
        select count(*)
        from   bricks b
        where  b.colour = c.colour
       ) brick#
from   COLORS c;
```

The SELECT clause is processed after FROM, meaning all the rows must be read from the COLORS table first, despite that step being lower in the plan.

Here, the order of operation is:

1. Traverse to the FROM clause and go to the first leaf – the COLORS table's TABLE ACCESS FULL, from step three in the execution plan.

2. This table's rows are then passed to the SELECT statement in step 0.

3. The subquery is run for each row, so the next one is the BRICKS table's TABLE ACCESS FULL in step two.

4. This table's rows are then passed to SORT AGGREGATE in step one.

5. Steps one and two are repeated for each row in step three. Again, an optimization exists, called scalar subquery caching, enabling the steps to be executed once per distinct value in the COLORS table.

The optimizer will always navigate a plan using a depth-first search, but how will you know if your plan is the best one, and how can you assist the optimizer in finding a better plan?

The first step is to see the number of rows the optimizer estimated would be processed at every step. Compare that to the actual number – if the estimates are not right, it's highly likely there is a better plan. If the estimates are right, but things are still running slow, check if any data structures can be created to give you quick access to your data.

Chapter 8

SQL Server Query Optimization Techniques

We can talk all we want about optimizing the database's performance, but the best way to do that is to ensure the design is right the first time. Best practice and facts should be the two main ingredients when you make architecture and design decisions – technical debt is reduced, along with the need to keep fixing things later down the line.

There are lots of ways we can tweak indexes, queries, and server settings to speed things up, but, more often than not, we are limited to what can be achieved in a timely and cost-effective way by the application design and database architecture. Often, it might look as though making good design at the outset a priority is costlier than being able to roll out new features quickly, but you pay a much higher price in the long run if you ignore it.

In this chapter, we will look at some of the design considerations in building tables, databases, and procedural TQSL. These are some ways you can improve performance over the long-term – spend the time at the start making good decisions and cut down the amount of work you have to do later on. Predicting how an application will behave in the future is not always easy when you are just starting to build it, but you can give it the best chance of succeeding.

You must have heard the old saying, "measure twice, cut once." That applies to most things, including application development. The sooner you accept that taking the time at the start to get it right will be cheaper in the long run, the sooner you can get on with building acceptable, fast-performing applications.

Understanding the Application

The first thing you need to do is understand the need for the application and its corresponding database. You should also consider these questions:

- What is the application for? What is its purpose, and what kind of data is involved?

- Who will be accessing the application – end-users on the internet or business employees? Is it four people, 40,000, or four million people?

- How is the application accessed? Via a mobile app, a web page, a reporting interface, or local software in the cloud or on a computer?

- Will app usage be heavier at certain times of the day? If so, do we need extra resources to copy at busier times? Can we do maintenance during quieter periods? What uptime do we expect?

If you can get an idea of what your database is for, you can make better predictions about its future and reduce the chances of mistakes at the start. If you know the quirks, such as busier and quieter periods, use of APIs or ORMs, you can better understand how the application and database interact. This means you can make better decisions around that usage.

More often than not, understanding the application allows us to make simple assumptions, removing the need to make tons of decisions. So, when you design new database objects, these are some of the things you consider to ensure fewer issues and faster queries later down the line:

Scalability

The first thing to consider is how much the application will grow in the future, along with its data. When you build and maintain data, how you do it is dependent on how big it will be. While you may start small, there is every chance it will expand in the future, which must be considered right at the start. More often than not, code is built and tested in controlled environments that do not reflect real production environments in terms of data flow. However, we should still be able to estimate an app's usage and common needs.

Then metrics can be inferred, including memory requirements, database size, throughput, and CPU. The hardware the database is going on must be sufficient for adequate performance, and inferring metrics means we can allocate the necessary resources. For example, if you had a 10 TB database, it won't run all that well on a server that only has 2 GB RAM. Likewise, high-traffic apps need faster network throughput and storage, not to mention fast SSDs. Databases can only perform as well as the slowest component – it's our job to ensure that component is fast enough to cope with the app.

Ask yourself if the data will grow in the future? If yes, how easy is it to expand the memory and storage if required? If downtime is not in the equation, consider different hardware configurations that will do one of two things (or both) – provide plenty of additional overhead right from the start or allow for smooth expansions to happen later. If you cannot estimate data growth, what about the customer or user count? Will they grow> If yes, you can use that to infer usage or data growth.

Licensing is also something that has to be considered – it isn't cheap to license a database. You need to compare the SQL server edition the database will function on with other versions that may be cheaper and do the same job. If your server is internal and has no customer-facing access, you may get away with using the Developer editions. Alternatively, consider the features offered by the Standard and Enterprise editions – which one offers the best for what you need it for? Getting the right edition at the start will ensure a hassle-free experience all the way through.

Finally, you must consider two more things right at the start – availability and disaster recovery. Often, developers forget about these things until it's too late. So, ask yourself what up-time you expect from the app. Ask yourself how quickly you should be able to recover from outages. And then ask yourself what level of data loss can be tolerated in the event of a disaster or outage. These are not easy questions to answer. More often than not, businesses want solid reassurances that there will be no data loss and no downtime but will quickly change their minds when they realize how expensive it will be to ensure those objectives are met. This an important consideration right at the start, before your app is released, as it ensures the technical capabilities can be met for the systems the app will live on. And it allows for future planning, avoiding the panic that tends to come with outages.

Data types

When you design your database, perhaps the most fundamental decision you should make is picking the correct data types. The right choices can ensure high performance and easy maintainability, while the wrong choices will just lead to more work later on.

Make sure you choose data types that are a natural fit for the data. For example, use the DATE data type for dates – it isn't a STRING or any other type. Bits should be a BIT type and not an INTEGER. Many years ago, data types were far more limited, and developers needed a certain amount of creativity to ensure they got the data they needed. This is just a hangover from those times – but it's a sensible one.

Choose the right precision, length, and size for the specific use case. You might think it useful to add extra precision, but don't do it if it isn't needed. It can confuse developers who need to know why a DECIMAL (18,4) has data that only has two decimal digits. In the same way, don't use DATETIME to store a TIME or DATE – this is also confusing and leads to poor data.

If you are unsure, use a standard. For example, ISO3166 can be used for countries, ISO5218 for genders, or ISO4217 for currencies. Doing this gives you a quick way to refer users or developers to the universal documentation to know what the data should look like, what is and isn't valid and how they should interpret it.

Don't store markup languages, such as JSON, XML, and HTML, in a database. It is expensive to store the data, even more so when you add having to retrieve and display it. Databases are there to store data and retrieve it. They are not there to generate web pages and documents.

Ensure date and time data is consistent over every table. If locations and time zones are important, model them using UTC or DATETIMEOFFSET. If you need to upgrade in the future to add support for time zones, it is much harder than if you add the support right at the start.

Times, dates, and durations are all different – ensure they are labeled so people can understand them. Store duration in one-dimensional scalar units, like minutes or seconds. If you store it as HH:MM:SS:mmm, it gets confusing and, when you need to use mathematical operations, they are not easy to manipulate.

NULLs

NULLs should be used when you need to model data non-existence meaningfully. Never make data up to complete NOT NULL columns, like -1 for integers, 1/1/1900 for dates, N/A for strings, or 00:00:00 for a time. NOT NULL is intended to mean that the application requires the column, and it should always have meaningful data in it.

NULL must have some kind of meaning, and this should be defined at the database design stage. For example, if you have "request_complete_date = NULL," it could indicate that a request is incomplete, while "Parent_id = NULL" could be indicating that an entity doesn't have a parent.

Extra normalization can eliminate NULL. For example, you could create a parent-child table for modeling an entity's hierarchical relationships. There could be some benefit to this where combined, the relationships become part of a critical component in an application's operations.

Normalization can be used to reverse NULLable columns being removed, especially where those columns are important to the application or only function properly with extra supporting schema. As always, though, using normalization purely for the sake of it is not good.

Be aware of NULL behavior because aggregate functions, inequalities, equalities, GROUP BY, and ORDER BY all treat NULL in different ways. SET ANSI_NULLS ON should always be set and, wherever you are performing an operation on a NULLable column, ensure NULL is checked for when needed.

Have a look at these two examples:

```
SELECT
    *
FROM Person.Person
WHERE Title = NULL

SELECT
    *
FROM Person.Person
WHERE Title IS NULL
```

They may look much the same, but both queries have different results. The first returns 0 rows, and the second returns 18,963 rows. This is because NULL isn't a value, which means it can't be treated as a string or number.

When you work with NULLable columns or check for NULL, you must always check and validate if you want NULL values included or excluded. And, rather than using <, >, =, etc., use IS NULL or IS NOT NULL.

SET ANSI_NULLS ON is an SQL Server default and must be left that way. If you change it, it affects the above behavior and definitely goes against the ANSI standards. It is far more preferable and scalable to build your code, so it handles NULL effectively.

Object names

It isn't easy to name things, but choosing useful names that describe the object ensures better readability. Developers can use the objects in their work easily and avoid mistakes.

Objects should be named for what they are. If it isn't plainly obvious, include a unit in the name – "duration_in_minutes" is far better than "duration" while "Length_meters" is better than just "Length."

If you have bit columns, name them in the positive and ensure the business use case is matched. For example, "is_flagged_for_deletion," "has_ten_kebabs," or "is_active." Try not to use negative columns as these are confusing. For example, "has_no_kebabs," or "is_not_active" can be confusing and lead to mistakes because they are not intuitive names. At the end of the day, database schema should be easy to understand – they should not require us to be puzzle-solvers to work out what they mean.

Some other things you should avoid are:

- **Using Shorthand and Abbreviations** – Very rarely do these not cause confusion. Should typing speed be a concern for those who don't smash out 100 wpm, think about using tools that provide auto-completion features, such as Intellisense.

- **Special Characters and Spaces** – These will confuse everyone, cause trouble with maintenance processes, and are nothing short of a nuisance in typing them properly. Stick with letters, numbers, and underscores, things everyone can understand and type easily.

- **Reserved Words** – If SSMS (SQL Server Management Studio) has something written in pink, white, or blue, you cannot use it – these are reserved, and using them elsewhere will be confusing, and you risk errors in the logical coding.

Consistency is incredibly valuable, and ensuring you use effective naming right from the start will cut the risk of fixing things later on. If your database uses many objects, you can use prefixes to ensure specific origins, types, and purposes of objects can be searched for. Alternatively, you may find it easier to use different schemas to divide different object types.

Starting off on the right foot, with good naming, reduces the risk of errors and speeds up development.

Old Data

When you create data, you should ask yourself a simple question – how long should the data exist for? Forever is, well, forever, and that's a long time; most data really doesn't need to exist for that long. Find out the retention policy for data or create one and ensure code is written to enforce it. Most businesses have retention policies that state the length of time data should be retained.

One of the best ways to improve the performance and cut the data footprint is to limit the data size. This is especially true where you have tables storing historical data. Smaller tables have smaller indexes, use less storage space, memory, and bandwidth usage. Seeks and scans are faster because the indexes are smaller, compact, and much easier to search.

Here are a few ways to deal with older data:

- **Delete it** – get rid of it forever. If it is allowed, this is the easiest solution.

- **Archive it** – copy the data to another location, i.e., a different partition, server, database, etc., and then delete it from the primary one.

- **Soft-delete it** – have a flag in place to indicate when your data is not relevant anymore, and normal processes can ignore it. This is one of the best solutions where filtered indexes, storage partitions, and other ways of segregating data can be leveraged.

- **Do nothing** – some data must be kept forever and, if that's the case, think about ways of making underlying structures more scalable to perform better later down the line. In this, you should consider the size the tables may grow to.

Data retention isn't just about OLTP (online transaction processing) tables. It may also have reporting data, data copies, backup files, and more. That's why it's important to apply retention policies to everything.

Cartesian Products – Cross Joins and the No Join Predicate

JOINS are used to join one or more data sets to newer ones and, when we bring them together, we use a set of 'keys' to join them. When data sets with no matching criteria are joined, it is known as a cartesian product or, better known, CROSS JOIN. However, while this is useful for generating the data an application needs, it can also hinder performance and cause issues with data quality when it is done unintentionally.

CROSS JOIN conditions may be generated in several ways:

- By using the CROSS JOIN operator
- By entering the wrong join criteria
- By omitting a join predicate unintentionally
- By forgetting to add a WHERE clause

The query below is an example of using the wrong join criteria:

```
SELECT
      Product.Name,
      Product.ProductNumber,
      ProductModel.Name AS
Product_Model_Name
FROM Production.Product
INNER JOIN Production.ProductModel
ON ProductModel.ProductModelID =
ProductModel.ProductModelID
WHERE Product.ProductID = 777;
```

We expect to see a single row with product data returned but, what we get is one row for every product model – that's 128 rows!

There are two hints here that something isn't as it should be. The first is the extremely large result, and the second is an index scan we didn't expect to show up in the execution plan. Examining the query closer shows us that an error was made on the INNER JOIN, and the table names were entered incorrectly:

```
INNER JOIN Production.ProductModel
ON ProductModel.ProductModelID =
ProductModel.ProductModelID
```

Because we put ProductModel on either side of the join, we told SQL Server that we didn't want Product joined to ProductModel. Instead, we wanted Product joined to the entire ProductModel. Why does this happen? Quite simply, because ProductModel.ProductModel is equal to itself and always will be. If we had input ON 1 = 1 as our join criteria, we would have got the same results.

This is an easy correction to make – the join criteria is adjusted so that Product is joined to ProductModel, as we wanted:

```
INNER JOIN Production.ProductModel
ON Product.ProductModelID =
ProductModel.ProductModelID
```

The query will now return the single row we expect, and an index scan is used on ProductModel.

In scenarios where a join predicate is wrong or missing, it isn't always to detect what is wrong. SQL Server won't always tell you and you might not get an error message or bad enough performance that you can't help but see it. So, to make it easier, the following tips will help you catch any bad joins before they cause problems:

- Ensure joins correlate to existing data sets with new tables. A CROSS JOIN should be used ONLY when you need it and very definitely intentionally, to inflate a data set's size or depth.

- Execution plans may warn you that a specific join has no predicate. Examine the execution plan carefully and, if you see such a warning, you know where to start looking.

- Look at the result set. You know what you expect to see so you know if it is too large or too small. Look to see whether tables are cross-joined across whole data sets, which will give you lots of extra rows of data – the bulk may be legitimate, but there will be extra added to the end.

- Does the execution plan indicate any odd index scans? What are they for? If they are for tables where you only expect to seek a few rows, like in lookup tables, you know something is wrong.

The standard rule of yellow and red exclamation marks should be adhered to. Anything with one of these beside it should be examined further, and, in this example, it would show us that no join predicate has been included. This is pretty easy to see in a short query, but larger ones, where many tables are involved, are not so easy and things can get buried – look at the execution plan for hints on where things have gone wrong.

Iteration

SQL Server is fully optimized for set-based operations. Reading and writing data row by row provides a far worse performance than in batches. Applications don't have that kind of constraint and tend to use iteration to parse the data sets.

You might think that there is no difference in the effort required to collect 100 rows from a table in a batch or one at a time, but you would be shocked. In reality, connecting to storage and reading into memory can take huge amounts of overhead, and the result is that 100 index seeks of individual times will take substantially longer and take more resources than one seek of all 100 rows:

```
DECLARE @id INT = (SELECT
MIN(BusinessEntityID) FROM
HumanResources.Employee)
WHILE @id <= 100
BEGIN
      UPDATE HumanResources.Employee
            SET VacationHours = VacationHours
+ 4
      WHERE BusinessEntityID = @id
      AND VacationHours < 200;

      SET @id = @id + 1;
END
```

This is a simple example. A loop is iterated through, an employee record updated, a counter incremented and repeated 99 times. It is slow, and the cost of the execution plan's I/O is shocking.

You might think, on glancing at the execution plan, that everything is ok. There is plenty of index seeks, and the individual read operations have a small cost attached. However, examine it closely, and we see that, while a couple of reads are relatively cheap, multiply it by 200, and you get the true cost. The same applies to the 100 separate execution plans generated for the update operations.

So, let's rewrite it so that all 100 rows are updated at the same time:

```
UPDATE HumanResources.Employee
    SET VacationHours = VacationHours + 4
WHERE VacationHours < 200
AND BusinessEntityID <= 100;
```

Now we only need five reads, not 200, and only one execution plan instead of 100.

SQL Server stored data in 8KB pages. When rows of data are read from memory or disk, 8KB pages are being read, no matter what size the data is. In the example we used above, the read operations didn't just read numeric values from disk and update them. To service the whole query, it had to read all the required 8KB pages.

Iteration is not seen very often, and by that, I mean it is there but hidden. This is because the operations are fast and cheap, making it hard to spot them when looking at trace data or extended events. You can catch iteration by looking for GOTO, WHILE loops, and CURSOR use, even when there isn't an outstanding poor performer in the operations.

Other tools can help us to avoid iteration. For example, when we insert new rows into tables, a common requirement is for the IDENTITY value to be returned immediately for the new rows. We do this by using SCOPE_IDENTITY() or @@IDENTITY, but neither of these functions is set-based. So, using them requires iteration through insert operations, individually, and the new identity values retrieved and processed after every loop. If we have more than a couple of rows, we will begin seeing similar inefficiencies to what we saw earlier

The code below shows you how OUTPUT INSERTED is used to retrieve bulk IDENTITY values without iteration:

```
CREATE TABLE #color
      (color_id SMALLINT NOT NULL
IDENTITY(1,1) PRIMARY KEY CLUSTERED,
color_name VARCHAR(50) NOT NULL,
datetime_added_utc DATETIME);
CREATE TABLE #id_values
      (color_id SMALLINT NOT NULL PRIMARY
KEY CLUSTERED, color_name VARCHAR(50) NOT
NULL);

INSERT INTO #color
      (color_name, datetime_added_utc)
OUTPUT INSERTED.color_id,
INSERTED.color_name
INTO #id_values
VALUES
      ('Red', GETUTCDATE()),
      ('Blue', GETUTCDATE()),
      ('Yellow', GETUTCDATE()),
      ('Brown', GETUTCDATE()),
```

```
        ('Pink', GETUTCDATE());

SELECT * FROM #id_values;

DROP TABLE #color;
DROP TABLE #id_values;
```

Here, new rows were inserted into #color using a set-based method. The new ids we inserted are then pulled into a temp table, along with color_name. Once they are in there, the values can be used in any operation we need them in without iterating individually through every INSERT operation.

Another useful method to reduce the requirement to iterate is the window functions. With these, we can pull sums, row counts, min and max values, and so much more without having to execute other queries or having to iterate manually through data windows:

```
SELECT
        SalesOrderHeader.SalesOrderID,
        SalesOrderDetail.SalesOrderDetailID,
        SalesOrderHeader.SalesPersonID,
        ROW_NUMBER() OVER (PARTITION BY SalesOrderHeader.SalesPersonID ORDER BY SalesOrderDetail.SalesOrderDetailID ASC) AS SalesPersonRowNum,
        SUM(SalesOrderHeader.SubTotal) OVER (PARTITION BY SalesOrderHeader.SalesPersonID ORDER BY SalesOrderDetail.SalesOrderDetailID ASC) AS SalesPersonSales
FROM Sales.SalesOrderHeader
INNER JOIN Sales.SalesOrderDetail
ON SalesOrderDetail.SalesOrderID = SalesOrderHeader.SalesOrderID
```

```
WHERE SalesOrderHeader.SalesPersonID IS NOT
NULL
AND SalesOrderHeader.Status = 5;
```

The results are a row-per-detail line, a running count of all the orders for each salesperson, and a running sales total.

Windows functions aren't terribly efficient, though. The query above needs some heavy lifting in the form of sort operations to get the results. However, although the cost isn't cheap, it still works out more efficient than iteration through iterative operations, such as orders, salespersons, etc., when dealing with large data sets.

Iteration isn't the only thing we have to avoid – we also need to steer clear of aggregation within queries, giving us the ability to select the columns we want freely, without worrying about constraints that come with GROUP BY and HAVING queries.

Don't get me wrong. It isn't always bad to use iteration because sometimes you will need all the databases on one server or all the servers on one list queried. You may also need to send emails, call stored procedures, or do other things that may be impossible or, at the very least, inefficient when using a set-based method. For these, you need to ensure adequate performance and limit how many times a loop is repeated, thus avoiding long-running jobs.

Encapsulation

When you write application code, you can use encapsulation to reuse code and make complicated interfaces simpler. When you package code into stored procedures, functions, or views, it makes it easier to offload the reusable code or critical business logic to a place where any code can call it when they need it.

This may sound great, but you can soon find performance failing when you use it too often. Chains of objects, linked by more encapsulated objects, get bigger and cause bottlenecks. For example, if you have one stored procedure calling another that uses a function that calls views, which, in turn, calls views, and so on. Sure, that might sound daft, but it happens, and it's common when we rely too much on nested stored procedures and views.

So, how does this affect performance? Here are some of the more common ways:

- We apply filters, joins, and subqueries that we really don't need

- We get columns returned that we don't need for a specified application

- CROSS JOINs, INNER JOINs, and filters force reads on tables we don't need for a specific operation

- The query size, which is the number of tables a query references, results in a less than sufficient execution plan

- Unclear query logic that isn't properly understood can lead to logical mistakes being made.

Here's a query where the simplest of intentions has the most complex of results:

```sql
SELECT
    BusinessEntityID,
    Title,
    FirstName,
    LastName
FROM HumanResources.vEmployee
WHERE FirstName LIKE 'E%'
```

At first look, we can see that the query pulls just four columns from the view named employee. We get the results we expected, but it takes longer to get there. The answer lies in the execution plan, which shows us that much was going on behind the scenes that we didn't know anything about. Unrequired tables were accesses, resulting in more reads than we needed being performed. That leads to the question of what is in the view called vEmployee? The following is that view's definition:

```sql
CREATE VIEW [HumanResources].[vEmployee]
AS
SELECT
    e.[BusinessEntityID]
    ,p.[Title]
    ,p.[FirstName]
    ,p.[MiddleName]
    ,p.[LastName]
    ,p.[Suffix]
    ,e.[JobTitle]
    ,pp.[PhoneNumber]
    ,pnt.[Name] AS [PhoneNumberType]
    ,ea.[EmailAddress]
    ,p.[EmailPromotion]
    ,a.[AddressLine1]
    ,a.[AddressLine2]
    ,a.[City]
```

```sql
      ,sp.[Name] AS [StateProvinceName]
      ,a.[PostalCode]
      ,cr.[Name] AS [CountryRegionName]
      ,p.[AdditionalContactInfo]
FROM [HumanResources].[Employee] e
      INNER JOIN [Person].[Person] p
      ON p.[BusinessEntityID] =
e.[BusinessEntityID]
      INNER JOIN
[Person].[BusinessEntityAddress] bea
      ON bea.[BusinessEntityID] =
e.[BusinessEntityID]
      INNER JOIN [Person].[Address] a
      ON a.[AddressID] = bea.[AddressID]
      INNER JOIN [Person].[StateProvince] sp
      ON sp.[StateProvinceID] =
a.[StateProvinceID]
      INNER JOIN [Person].[CountryRegion] cr
      ON cr.[CountryRegionCode] =
sp.[CountryRegionCode]
      LEFT OUTER JOIN [Person].[PersonPhone] pp
      ON pp.BusinessEntityID =
p.[BusinessEntityID]
      LEFT OUTER JOIN
[Person].[PhoneNumberType] pnt
      ON pp.[PhoneNumberTypeID] =
pnt.[PhoneNumberTypeID]
      LEFT OUTER JOIN [Person].[EmailAddress] ea
      ON p.[BusinessEntityID] =
ea.[BusinessEntityID];
```

Here, you can see many basic data about employees, but we can also see loads of other tables that are not related to our query and that we didn't need to access. In some circumstances, the performance we got would probably be acceptable, but you must fully understand the objects you are using so you know how to use them more effectively. If we needed better performance, our query could be rewritten like this:

```
SELECT
    e.BusinessEntityID,
    p.Title,
    p.FirstName,
    p.LastName
FROM HumanResources.Employee e
INNER JOIN Person.Person p
ON p.BusinessEntityID = e.BusinessEntityID
WHERE FirstName LIKE 'E%'
```

Here we are only accessing the required tables, resulting in the reads being halved and the execution plan being a great deal simpler.

Like many other things we've discussed here, encapsulation isn't always bad. However, when dealing with data, over-encapsulation can be dangerous. Use the following guidelines to keep performance issues to a minimum when you nest database objects:

- Where it is possible, don't nest a view within a view. That way, code visibility is improved, and there is less chance of misunderstanding a given view's contents.

- If you can get away with it, don't nest functions. Doing so leads to confusion and a whole host of challenging issues concerning performance.

- Steer clear of any trigger that does too much business logic or calls stored procedures. Be aware that even nested triggers are dangerous, and operations inside triggers can fire off more triggers, complicating things even further.

- You must understand what the functionality is of any defined object – a view, a trigger, a function, a stored procedure, etc. – before you use it. That way, you won't find yourself misunderstanding what they are for.

A good way to use code reuse for better maintainability is to store frequently used and important TSQL inside views, procedures, or functions. Be cautious at all times and make sure encapsulated objects don't become too complex. When you nest objects multiple layers deep, you can significantly impact performance. When you troubleshoot queries that are causing issues, look at the objects – that way, you can clearly see any functions, views, triggers, or stored procedures that are part of the execution.

OLTP vs. OLAP

Typically, we access data for one of two reasons – analytical/reporting or transactional. Databases can be optimized effectively to handle both of these scenarios, but how we tune each for performance is very different and must be considered when designing the elements of your database.

OLTP

OLTP stands for Online Transaction Processing. It refers to workloads where data is written/read for interactive business use. Typically, an OLTOP workload is characterized by these patterns:

- Lots of additional writes, including updating or deleting rows, adding new data, etc.

- Many more interactive operations where apps or websites are being logged into and the data viewed or modified. This covers the common business uses.

- Operations carried out on small row counts, including updating orders, adding new contacts, viewing recent store transactions, and so on. Often, these operations are done on recent or current data.

- Lots more tables and joins are included in the queries.

- Timeliness is a critical factor, and latency is never tolerated because users should never be kept waiting.

- Higher transaction counts, but transactions are smaller.

OLTP environments are relational. Indexes are aimed more at searches, updates, or core application operations. Generally, an OLTP process will ensure data integrity and rely on it. At times, foreign keys may be needed for this, along with default constraints, check constraints, and triggers to help guarantee the integrity of real-time data.

OLAP

Standing for Online Analytical Processing, this refers to the search or reporting environments, typically used when huge amounts of data must be crunched. This includes data mining, reporting, and analytics. Common OLAP workload features include:

- Typically, an OLAP workload is read-only and writes only happen during specified update and load times.

- Many OLAP operations are scheduled to run or automated, being delivered to users at specified times. Often, these are used when insight is needed into a business to help with making the right decisions.

- OLAP operations can be used on huge amounts of data, including year-on-year data crunching, monitoring trending levels of spending over a specific quarter, or other tasks that may need longer histories pulled to be completed.

- Tables are wider, and there are fewer of them, which means fewer lookups or joins are needed to generate reports.

- Users don't have to sit and wait for results as they are delivered asynchronously, such as by email or a file. If a user does have to wait, they may find a delay because of the sheer size of the data. Where timeliness is critical in a report, the data-crunching can be done ahead of time to be ready when the results are needed.

- They typically have fewer transactions, but each one is much larger.

OLAP environments tend to be flatter and not so relational. Data gets created in OLTP environments before being passed to the OLAP environments, where the analytics happen. The result of this is that data integrity is often assumed to be established already, meaning that keys, constraints, and other similar checks can be omitted on some occasions.

Where data is transformed or crunched, it can be validated later and not in real-time like we have to do with OLTP. OLAP data invites creativity, depending on the speed the results are required, how current the data must be, and how much history is required.

Keeping OLTP and OLAP Separate

Because OLAP and OLTP have significantly different requirements, we should keep analytical and transactional systems as far apart as we can. One of the biggest reasons is that applications tend to slow down. We resort to NOLOCK hints when we run bulky reports or large search queries against applications in a transactional production environment. The higher the transaction counts go and the more data we get, the more clashes we can expect to see between transactional and analytical operations. We can expect to see the following:

- When you carry out large report or search runs, and users are attempting data updates, you can expect deadlocks, blocking, and locking.

- Tables will be over-indexed to try to service many types of queries.

- Latency

- Query hints will be used to try to get around performance issues.

- Constraints and foreign keys are removed to speed writes up.

- More hardware is given to the server to try to increase performance.

The best solution is to know the difference between the two types of workload when you design your application and ensure they are separated right from the start. Often, personnel, cost, or time constraints get in the way of this, and it doesn't happen.

No matter how severe things are or how long the problem has been going on, the only solution is to separate operations per their type. The first step is to create a new environment where OLAP data is stored, and you can do this using log shipping, Always-On, data copying at the storage level, ETL processes, and lots of other methods that copy the OLTP data.

Once done, you can offload operations over time. If you ease into it, you have more QA time, and you can use more caution while the business familiarizes itself with the new tools. As operations gradually move over to a new data store, reporting indexes can be removed from the OLTP source, which can then be optimized for servicing OLTP workloads. In the same way, we can optimize the OLAP data store to do the analytical work, which means you can remove constraints, flatten tables, remove OLTP indexes, and whatever else is needed to speed it up.

The more degrees of separation you have between processes, the easier you will find it to optimize the environments for what they are best at. Not only do you get better performance, but you also find that features are easier to develop. It is much easier to write a table purely for reporting than writing a query against a transactional table. In the same way, when you can update the code, knowing that your database won't have any huge reports running against it, you can eliminate most of the performance issues that come with mixed environments.

Triggers

In themselves, triggers are not a bad thing. However, the performance issues come with serious overuse because the triggers get put on tables, firing after or in place of updates, inserts, and/or deletes.

Where triggers can cause serious performance issues is when you have far too many of them. When you update a table, and it results in deletes, updates, and inserts against dozens of other tables, it can be challenging to keep track of performance. It takes time to find out which code is responsible, often involving a great deal of searching before you locate it.

Often, we use triggers to implement application or business logic, but we don't build or optimize relational databases for this. Typically, an application should take on as much of this work as it can but, when it can't, stored procedures should be used in place of triggers where possible.

Triggers tend to be integrated into the calling transaction, which is where the danger of using them lies. One write operation can become multiple operations, with other processes having to wait until every trigger has been fired successfully.

Some of the best practices you should follow are:

- Only use a trigger when absolutely necessary, never to save time or for convenience.

- Don't use a trigger that will call more of them, as this can result in critical IO amounts or complicated query paths that are tough to debug.

- Disable server trigger recursion, which is enabled by default. When you let a trigger call itself, be it indirectly or directly, it results in instability or, worse, infinite loops.

- Keep it simple. If you need to use a trigger, ensure it only executes one purpose.

Conclusion

Thank you for taking the time to read my guide on optimizing your SQL queries. Query optimization is a massive topic and, if you are not focused, you can soon find it overwhelms you—the first step in dealing with query performance issues to look for the easy options. Find the areas where latency is likely to be an issue and deal with them first. For example, stored procedures can be thousands of lines long, but you probably only need to deal with one to solve the issue. In a scenario like this, finding the parts of your script that consume huge amounts of resources and have a high cost attached can help narrow the search down, allowing you to solve the issue rather than waste time looking for it.

In this guide, I have tried to give you a starting point to dealing with performance and latency issues. Be aware that optimizing queries will sometimes need extra resources, like adding extra indexes, but this can sometimes lead to no additional costs being added. If you can rewrite your query to improve the performance, resource consumption can be reduced at no extra cost, apart from a little of your time. As a result, optimization can be a great way to save costs. Not only that, but you also get the satisfaction of improving a process without extra costs to anyone else in the equation.

We also looked at common mistakes coders make when writing their queries, leading to a loss of performance. Because these mistakes are fairly easy to find without spending hours on research, this knowledge can then be used to improve how quickly we respond to latency and performance problems. While I couldn't possibly cover everything, I have given you a good starting point in finding where your scripts are weak.

Whether you clean up WHERE clauses and joins, or break your query down into smaller ones, when you focus your QA, evaluation, and testing processes, you can improve the quality of your queries and results, as well as speeding things up.

Troubleshooting performance issues is challenging. There are no two ways about it. It is also frustrating and time-consuming, but the easiest way to avoid it is to design and build an optimized database from the outset, avoiding the need to fix things later.

By understanding the information about an application about how it is used, your design architecture decisions will be smarter, allowing a more scalable database to be built with better performance.

Good luck in troubleshooting your SQL queries. Hopefully, the information in this book will make your job much easier.

References

"Database SQL Tuning Guide." *Docs.oracle.com*, docs.oracle.com/database/121/TGSQL/tgsql_optcncpt.htm#TGSQL194.

"Introduction to the Optimizer." *Docs.oracle.com*, docs.oracle.com/cd/B10500_01/server.920/a96533/optimops.htm. Accessed 5 July 2021.

"Performance Tuning SQL Queries | Advanced SQL - Mode Analytics." *Mode Resources*, 23 May 2016, mode.com/sql-tutorial/sql-performance-tuning/.

Plans, Reading Oracle Explain, and Part 1: The Basics says. "Reading Oracle Explain Plans, Part 2: The RBO and the CBO." *SolarWinds*, 26 Nov. 2012, logicalread.com/reading-oracle-explain-plans-part-2-h01/#.YOJyk-gzZPY. Accessed 5 July 2021.

Pollack, Ed. "Query Optimization Techniques in SQL Server: The Basics." *SQL Shack - Articles about Database Auditing, Server Performance, Data Recovery, and More*, 30 May 2018, www.sqlshack.com/query-optimization-techniques-in-sql-server-the-basics/.

"RBO,CBO - Ask TOM." *Asktom.oracle.com*, asktom.oracle.com/pls/apex/asktom.search?tag=rbocbo. Accessed 5 July 2021.

"SQL Query Optimization: Level up Your SQL Performance Tuning." *Blog.toadworld.com*, blog.toadworld.com/sql-query-optimization-level-up-your-sql-performance-tuning. Accessed 5 July 2021.

"Understanding a SQL Server Execution Plan - ." *Docs.rackspace.com*, docs.rackspace.com/blog/understanding-a-sql-server-execution-plan/.

CPSIA information can be obtained
at www.ICGtesting.com
Printed in the USA
BVHW052001060623
665497BV00015B/939

9 781955 786621